The 2nd Language of Leadership™

The 2nd Language of Leadership ™

Michael P. Quirk
Patricia M. Fandt
University of Washington, Tacoma

LEA LAWRENCE ERLBAUM ASSOCIATES, PUBLISHERS
2000 Mahwah, New Jersey   London

Copyright © 2000 by Michael P. Quirk and Margaret M. Quirk.
All rights reserved. No part of this book may be reproduced in any form, by photostat, microfilm, retrieval system, or any other means, without the prior written permission of the publisher.

Lawrence Erlbaum Associates, Inc., Publishers
10 Industrial Avenue
Mahwah, New Jersey 07430-2262

Cover design by Kathryn Houghtaling Lacey

Library of Congress Cataloging-in-Publication Data

Quirk, Michael P.
  The 2nd language of leadership / Michael P. Quirk, Patricia M. Fandt.
    p. cm.
  Includes bibliographical references and index.
  ISBN 0-8058-3357-9 (pbk. : alk. paper)
  1. Leadership. 2. Management. I. Title: Second language of leadership. II. Fandt, Patricia M. III. Title.
HD57.7.Q57 2000
658.4'092—dc21   99-088672
                                            CIP

Books published by Lawrence Erlbaum Associates are printed on acid-free paper, and their bindings are chosen for strength and durability

Printed in the United States of America
10 9 8 7 6 5 4 3 2 1

Contents

	About the Authors	vii
	Preface	ix
Chapter 1	The Popcorn Chronicles	1
Chapter 2	Personality: An Organizing Role in How Leaders Succeed and Fail	14
Chapter 3	Personality Fundamentals and the Big 5 Concept	25
Chapter 4	Three Languages of Leadership	39
Chapter 5	2nd Language Challenges	51
Chapter 6	Leadership Development Strategies	60
Chapter 7	Learning to Lead: The Good News	75
Chapter 8	2nd Language Goal Setting	84
Chapter 9	3rd Language	95

Chapter 10	Where We've Been and Where We're Going	**106**
	Appendix	**114**
	References	**120**
	Index	**124**

About the Authors

Michael P. Quirk is a clinical psychologist from Seattle, Washington and is the creator of the 2nd Language of Leadership model of personality and leadership development. Dr. Quirk is also the director of Behavioral Health for the Population Services Division of Group Health Cooperative of Puget Sound. Dr. Quirk received his doctorate and master's degrees at Washington State University. He is both a diplomate of the American Board of Professional Psychology in clinical psychology and a fellow of the Society for Personality Assessment.

Patricia M. Fandt is a professor of management and the founding director of the Business School at the University of Washington, Tacoma. Dr. Fandt earned her PhD at Texas A&M University and her MBA at the University of West Florida. She has authored or co-authored six books focused on management and managerial skills. Prior to her academic career, Dr. Fandt spent 12 years in industry with Proctor & Gamble and 3M.

Preface

An unfortunate reality is that more than half of the people who aspire to leadership roles fail. Generally, they fail not because of lack of technical expertise, nor because of an inability to conceptualize the job that needs to be done. Mostly the failures have to do with individuals not knowing how to bridge the gap between who they are as a person and what type of behavior is expected of them on the job. This lack of knowledge and understanding is more significant than being deficient in highly specialized expertise. To most organizations that are continually searching for individuals who have competencies beyond expertise in a specific discipline, this fact comes as no surprise. The competencies organizations are looking for in individuals are often referred to as human behavior skills that include the ability to understand oneself and others. When leaders do have that personal knowledge and ability, they are instinctively aware of it. Despite not having complete alignment between their personality and the requirement of the job, leaders make the necessary adaptations and compensations. Similar to learning a new language, they may not have a fully natural command of the leadership situation, yet they have acquired a sufficiently fluent language of the necessary behaviors that more than gets them by.

The objective of this book is to help you acquire and integrate information about yourself and your personality on one hand and the demands of being a leader on the other. The goal here is to introduce you to the 2nd Language of Leadership, which is a new way of thinking about personality, leadership and the linkages to success on the job. Your leadership decisions based on reasonable judgment and adequate information can regularly result in success that should sustain you in your role. Leadership is more a set of behaviors that you learn rather than fully developed gifts with which you are born. The focus of this book, and more fundamentally the purpose of the 2nd Language model is to make it possible for most individuals to learn quickly and easily how to gather relevant personal information to increase their leadership effectiveness.

Essentially, we are all desperate for good leaders. Leaders have a major influence over job satisfaction, determine the success or failure of our business efforts, and set the course for national security and prestige in the world. Leadership matters! We commonly define a good leader as a person with an active, adaptive form of integrity. Integrity can be defined in behavioral terms that track with how we think of personality. Most people have enough flexibility in their personality to increase their positive adaptation in life. Similarly, leaders can learn to bring more integrity to their work.

The complication lies in how to learn about yourself with regard to personality and integrity. What is the personality fit or conflict with the job that you are being asked to do? Most of us find ourselves in leadership roles because we were considered to have certain strengths as a leader. However, virtually none of us would say that we are superb leaders all the time, across every situation. Most of us have one or two noteworthy natural strengths. Should we go beyond these, they must be acquired like another language.

For example, you may be extraordinarily open to experience and be considered a visionary; very considerate and agreeable; highly conscientious and reliable; dependable and be counted on to get the job done. You may be extraverted and charismatic, or be a person with a remarkable presence of emotional well-being. As it works out, those five characteristics cover the foundation of what studies have shown are involved in being perceived as a person with leadership integrity. They are also the same set of five characteristics that make up the scientifically robust Big 5 theory of personality. The good news for you is that you only have to be gifted at one of the five to be an effective leader. Yes, it is like baseball in the sense that batting .200 makes you a respectable player.

The challenge is in acquiring this information in ways that are useful to you. That difficulty was the reason for putting together the 2nd Language model, presenting it in a workshop format, and now responding to participants asking for more about it in writing by producing this book.

Our own previous efforts to piece together the relationship of person–behavior and leadership situations set us on a long journey of considering a wide range of books, surveys, profiles, inventories and conferences or workshops. Often, what we found was opinion without any scientific foundation. Or if there was an empirical basis, the information was converted into lists of behaviors or principles that did not consider either the personality of the leader or whether information or action was most important to the leader.

In our experience, if leadership effectiveness material is offered only in an action mode, you can lose upward to half of your audience. The personality tests used range from too positive (Myers–Briggs) to too negative (Minnesota Multiphasic Personality Inventory). Conferences often seemed geared toward both affluent and well-established senior leaders with price tags in the $500+ per day price range.

This is not to say that there is not good leadership information available. There is! *The Leadership Challenge* and *Managing at the Speed of Change* are both excellent books that lay out the broad strokes of the leadership process, clarify how to form teams, and make decisions. Organizations such as the Center for Creative Leadership are very solid and have an international reputation. Bernard Bass' scientific studies of leadership are outstanding. He, better than anyone else, has clarified how to bridge the management–leadership polarity with his work on transformational and transactional leadership. In other words, leaders who inspire, intellectually challenge, and create individual opportunity for their followers (i.e., transformational leadership) produce high-performing organizations to the extent that they can convert their high purpose into specific performance expectations that are rewarded (i.e., transactional leadership).

Notwithstanding all this progress, the missing thread in the leadership fabric is one of looking for information that is specific to you as a person so that you can intelligently think about how you match with and can get prepared for the particular leadership situation that you are dealing with now. As Albert Einstein was reputed to have said, the key to solutions is to ask the right questions. This book inquires about personality tests that are available to assess the alignment with leadership and, once those tests are identified, questions what strategies can be used to increase leadership effectiveness.

The answer to the first inquiry is the Mini Markers from the Big 5 personality theory. It is included in the book as part of the 2nd Language model, and you can take and score the inventory yourself. Alternately you can ask your leadership team members to also complete the inventory with you as the leader. Another Big 5 test, the NEO–PI is reviewed as well. Relative to the second question about strategies, the 2nd Language of Leadership model advises you to use your strengths both in themselves and as leverage points; complement your collegial relationships with those people who give you balance and breadth; and choose not to take on work that is incompatible with your strengths, motivations, and values. Yes, the ideas are simple, and are actually consistent with what we know about how people change in general in and out of professional counseling relationships. However, as we need not tell you, at the personal level of "you and me," this is hard-won simplicity.

With these preliminary comments as a reference point concerning how the 2nd Language model originated, we proceed with the content and organization of the book. What you will notice throughout is that we have not prescribed a theory of leadership to you. Beyond the most general of thoughts that leadership is about making sense of situations, motivating people, and accomplishing work, you are completely at liberty to use any specific definition of leadership that functions for you.

The foundation for this book is that there is a relation between this broad definition of leadership and the Big 5 personality structure. Essentially, the factors and relationships are Openness–Making sense, Extraversion/Consideration/Emotional Well-being–Motivating others, and Conscientiousness–Accomplishing work. Therein you can build, within reason, your desired leadership pattern. Please note, personality relates to both the average person's proxy for leadership including integrity and to our operational definition of making sense, motivating, and accomplishing.

In this regard, the 2nd Language approach is like a toolbox of techniques that are used to craft your desired behavior pattern. It is not a cookbook or a blue print that is limited to one particular school of thought about leadership. On the contrary, it is broadly based and has been designed to be applied so that it allows for tailoring of your unique personality with the particular situation you are encountering.

For example, a leader may be a visionary but not very conscientious in a work situation that calls for more in the way of maintenance than innovation. This type of awareness becomes clear when you complete the Mini Markers and fill out the 2nd Language of Leadership Questionnaire found in the Appendix. The questionnaire asks you about what the leadership situation involves, and what about it is easy and hard for you to do. Gradually, you get into focus and prepare for this particular sense making/motivating/accomplishing work situation. With this preparation, you will be at the threshold of considering the response options that are working from strengths, complement those with the personal strengths of others, or pass up this leadership opportunity. The book provides you with multiple examples that take you from start to finish in this process.

Within the framework of the 10 chapters, our goals in the book are as follows:

1. Promote a shared recognition of the role that personality plays in leadership by reviewing a case study of a representative leadership situation that both identifies familiar personal struggles and organizational changes (chap. 1).
2. Offer a way of thinking about how personality in general and the Big 5 in particular fills in the gaps and connects the pieces when it comes to how people become effective leaders (chap. 2 and 3).

PREFACE   xiii

3. Illustrate how, within the Big 5 framework, to use the 2nd Language approach to leverage natural personality strengths (1st Language of Leadership) and manage weaknesses in an effort to build greater leadership effectiveness (chap. 4 and 5).
4. Make available 2nd Language tools including effective intervention strategies and goal-setting techniques based on enabling philosophies to understand what makes this approach accessible and practical to use (chap. 6, 7, and 8).
5. Reassure that most leadership failures are reversible (3rd Language of Leadership) and that through using the 2nd Language approach, these inevitable and sometimes necessary setbacks afford clarity about how to use your style to the best advantage (chap. 9).

Each chapter can stand alone and yet is sequentially related to the larger framework of the book. At the beginning of each chapter, we have included a brief synopsis to help you select key concepts to concentrate on now or to use as a review.

Chapter 10 provides an overall summary and a brief glimpse of the next steps beyond reading this book. At the back of the book, there is a Reference guide for your review of what was considered in developing this model and for additional reading purposes. Finally, below, please read the introductory synopsis of the main points of this book.

SYNOPSIS

1. Leadership is the act of making sense of situations and motivating people to accomplish work.
2. Leadership is a set of behaviors that flow out of our personalities, and in the Big 5 theory, behaviors are organized into

   - Openness: making sense,
   - Extraversion: taking the message to the world,
   - Agreeableness: considering the needs of workers,
   - Adaptiveness: keeping emotionally steady, and
   - Conscientiousness: following through.

3. Leadership effectiveness occurs when you

   - use your strengths for leverage,
   - partner with others to complement weaknesses, and
   - choose to maintain compatibility of personality and leadership.

4. Leadership effectiveness outcomes maximize when you

   - are aware of the range of your personality,
   - acknowledge the gift of your strengths, and
   - employ the transforming power of life values.

ACKNOWLEDGMENTS

I want to thank my wife Margaret and our sons Dan and John for their support of the personal time I devoted to developing this idea about leadership and personality. I want to thank my co-workers past and present who have provided me the opportunity to learn in a tangible way what leadership means in my own life. I am especially grateful to my colleagues at Group Health Cooperative of Puget Sound, and particularly to Rich Goepfert, Marcy Maurer, and Al Truscott—all of whom expressed a belief in me and my potential to be a leader. I want to thank all the scientists and practitioners who have established the foundation of psychological and leadership thought, from which I have developed the 2nd Language of Leadership model. I particularly want to acknowledge Phil Erdberg, Patricia Fandt, and Gerard Saucier.

—MPQ

To my family and colleagues, thank you for your continuing support and confidence in my endeavors; to Michael Quirk for involving me in the early stages of his model; and to Anne Duffy, our editor at LEA, thank you.

—PMF

The Popcorn Chronicles

Synopsis

The Popcorn Chronicles is a case study of leadership challenges during a transition time in an organization. It describes a common situation in today's work world—the need to increase profitability. Based on the case study, a series of questions are raised about the personality aspects of leadership behavior. These questions set the stage for the development of *The 2nd Language of Leadership* outlined in the remainder of the book.

SETTING THE STAGE

We considered several options while beginning this book and making the case for the viability for the 2nd Language of Leadership. We could have reviewed the literature and called out the limitations of other personality and behavioral approaches. Although that has merit, it is at best argumentative and at worst negative. We could go right into the didactics of personality and leadership theory, behavior change mechanics, and goal setting and achievement. Although that is covered in the book, we doubted it would be the most engaging draw into the 2nd Language model. What did seem most accessible was to tell a story, to let you see if it is representative of your world and whether the embedded principles of this model come to life in ways that are credible to your living the leadership life.

We have titled the story The Popcorn Chronicles. The basis for the unusual name becomes obvious as you read the story. The story is a senior manager's retrospective reflection on his interactions with a middle manager. The senior manager has been required to assure that all of the businesses that report to him become profit centers.

As has been observed in many industries, the pendulum has now shifted to a decentralized emphasis on the importance of successful local management as measured by a positive financial margin. Along with a concern for the bottom line, the focus rests on high customer satisfaction with both the quality of service and the product that is being delivered. Within private industry, for example, restaurant franchises, hotel/motel chains, computer/software companies, or insurance organizations, this goal serves the needs of the shareholders who want dividends and the owner whose capitalistic motive is to maximize profit. As for the public domain, similar themes are present. For example, the exclusivity of the U.S. Post Office has been usurped by entrepreneurial mail service companies. This has stimulated U.S. Postal managers to improve performance or relinquish the familiar trappings of control and achievement as represented by budget size, number of employees, and praise and acknowledgment for a job well done. Colleges and universities that have traditionally been nonprofit institutions, whether state assisted or privately funded, are discovering a competitive force in the marketplace with a new focus on higher education as a profit center and a service provided to the paying customer. Like their civilian counterparts, even the Veterans Administration and the Army Hospitals are transitioning into managed-care businesses expected to survive and succeed within a fixed amount of resources deemed to be adequate by the actuaries. This is the world in which most of us live. It is a departure from government organizations operating in an annual cost plus budgeting culture. Private industry's tolerance for cross-subsidizing low performers has declined significantly.

It is within this new business culture that this leadership story unfolds. The organization is a chain of coffee shops called Roberto's and our protagonist is Joe Barett. The owner of Roberto's, Michelle Roberto, had created the business with the objective of distinguishing it from the fast-paced "get in, get out" competition by hiring warm, friendly, customer-oriented managers. Three years after founding the business, she had built 60 stores, with 30 in each of two northeast cities. Without a great deal of revenue targeting, only about half of the stores in each of the cities were making a profit.

Joe's previous job included the introduction of accessories into the coffee shops in order to leverage coffee drinkers into purchasing additional items. He was remarkably successful at anticipating what people might be willing to buy in addition to a cup of coffee and a pastry when they come into the store. Joe's accessories had contributed substantially to the bottom line.

Based on this success and in consideration of the owner's need to develop this relatively new business into a money maker rather than a money loser, Joe was seen as an employee with ambition and potential for greater opportunities. As a success-minded owner, Michele decided to promote Joe and assign him one city and a total of 30 stores. She reasoned that if Joe could lead up one effort well, he could do the same with a broader range of responsibilities.

Joe was promoted from an organization-wide product-line manager to a regional vice president with control over all store managers. In this position, he was accountable to Michelle Roberto for the financial improvements of each store in his region. Particularly challenging for Joe was the need to change the store managers' primary mindset of promoting their stores as a friendly gathering place for people in the community to a situation where the stores were both friendly and profitable.

The specific story has to do with Joe's relationship with Dianne Sparks, who was the manager of one of the largest and oldest stores. Dianne's shop was very popular, yet it was consistently in the red. Six months into Joe's new job, he began to see both acceptance and progress with 10 of the 15 stores that had previously been money losers. However, with Dianne's store the financial performance had not changed. Joe was far from convinced that his expectations had been heard and accepted by Dianne. In the following, Joe tells the story in his own words.

JOE'S STORY

I had heard a lot about Dianne Sparks from the time I had joined Roberto's. Dianne's shop, previously called Old Town Coffee, had been in existence for many years before Michele started the company.

The store, somewhat smaller then, had a unique personality where rich, exotic coffee smells in a well-lit, open setting created a warm, inviting atmosphere. Michelle had observed Dianne's interactions with employees and customers in a way that conveyed a sense of consideration and well-being. In addition to unusually high quality coffee, the configuration of the shop's space and assorted tables and chairs seemed to encourage people to sit down and take a break from the demands of home and work. In the past, the shop was one of three commonly owned interlocking businesses: The coffee shop, an art gallery, and a book store were all located on the first floor of a restored, historic brick building. Apparently Dianne had never made a profit, but the prior owner of all three shops was convinced that Old Town Coffee was a magnet that brought art and book-oriented folk to him over the competition. When the original owner sold this set of shops, Michelle purchased Old Town Coffee as a stand-alone business.

What made my job especially difficult in assuring the necessary turnaround for Dianne's store was her revered status with staff, customers, and Michelle. In essence, she was much loved and implicitly trusted, but she was not doing her job. It was obvious that Michelle wanted Dianne to turn the corner to profit, yet she didn't want (and given her executive status, didn't need) to take on Dianne herself. After all, Dianne's shop was the inspirational prototype in Michelle's business plan characterized by the slogan "Enjoy your coffee in a relaxed atmosphere."

As I considered what I could bring to this new challenge, I realized that I had achieved much of my success by being single-mindedly driven to achieve my stated goals. I believe in high quality products and excellent customer service, yet unlike Dianne, no one ever accused me of being warm and relaxed. I was glad that I had a boss like Michelle who valued my contributions to Roberto's Coffee Shops, and I was stimulated by the regional management promotion. However, I had my private doubts about how good a match I was for this new job. Although 10 of the 15 money-losing stores had begun a positive revenue trend, the net balance of my 30 shops was still in the red. I was concerned about the handful of older shops, larger than the others and carrying proportionately more expense, which were very much steeped in the relaxed culture that Dianne symbolized.

Over the course of my 15 years of working life, I had enjoyed good relationships with the relatively small sales teams that I had lead. We tended to be like-minded, yet I didn't stay with any group very long. My goals have been to move up the organizational ladder, motivated in part, to be frank, by the prestige and money that such advancements represent. Although my skill set as a leader was proven, I had no history of success (or failure) with the sort of transitional change that was represented in working with Dianne's group and the others like hers.

Gradually, it became clearer to me that the principal challenge in achieving success in my new role was finding the way to get Dianne on track. I decided that getting Dianne to make the necessary accommodations in business thinking would have a domino effect on the other shops, and then I would make it okay. The very unhappy downside of this thinking was that if I could not make this transition happen, I would most certainly fail. That thought was quite unsettling.

As I prepared to speak to Dianne, I spent some time thinking about our interactions to date and how they had gone. I originally met Dianne during my occasional visits to her shop when I was peddling my product line of accessories. I found her to be uniformally gracious in receiving me, but not especially engaged or enthusiastic about the various books, compact discs, coffee mugs, or espresso machines I was introducing. I enjoyed my time in the shop where, as was their wont, I was accepted in a pleasant, welcoming fashion. My accessories sold acceptably well, although I never heard the employees mention or recommend any of these products to customers.

When I was selected as the regional manager, Michelle went with me to all the stores including Dianne's. Michelle announced to the assembled staff that I represented a key link to a successful future where a good cup of coffee, a relaxed atmosphere, and profit could all be aligned. Staff in most of the shops seemed intrigued and encouraged by the introduction. Dianne's group, although characteristically warm and accepting of us as people, didn't seem to signal any sense of urgency, necessity, or excitement in association with our message.

I subsequently established a regular meeting time with groups of five to seven managers who had shops contiguous to one another. I also established a quarterly "sit down" with Dianne and the others to track their progress. Actually, because I had a sense that the change in culture might be particularly difficult for Dianne and her group, I had met with them and gave them a presentation above and beyond the initial introduction that Michelle had arranged. The essence of my message was that although Roberto's had promise as a business, the store simply would not succeed without all the shops carrying the weight of their expenses and producing a profit margin. I provided Dianne and her staff with seasonal charts of historical financial performance, along with marketing strategies for bringing in existing and potential clientele for more regular and expanded use of our services.

I spent a great deal of time explaining how to make customers aware of our accessory products and work site coffee service. In addition, I focused on the achievable goal of closing the gap between current and desired performance. Dianne was quiet but polite during the presentations. In short, I had delivered the message, and it was difficult to imagine that any reasonable person would not move quickly into action mode to make the needed adjustments in business practice.

Six months later, Dianne's financial performance remained flat with no appreciable change. This was dumbfounding to me. It was as if Dianne and her coworkers didn't believe or care that they would fail as a business and lose their jobs. I both believed and cared about this fate, and it was not one I wanted to accept. It became clear that Dianne, although a nice person, lacked the personal strengths I possessed myself, including being realistic, ambitious, and, if necessary, aggressive. Emboldened by my view that Dianne's deficiencies could cost me my job as well as hers, I determined to meet with her and her staff, repeat my prior presentation, and raise the fear level to get them moving in the right direction.

I called Dianne and told her to expect me at their monthly 2-hour staff meeting. I gave her the range of my thinking. She replied that she thought it would be helpful if we met face-to-face in the next several days to get ready for my visit. Although I had no confidence that such a meeting would be useful to me, I could not think of a reason not to meet, so I agreed to do so. I had more or less decided that the necessary adjustments would occur in her shop despite her and that it was essentially my job to get people on board and activated. In other words, Dianne could be relied on to be a warm person liked by staff and customers, but she certainly was not going to take the local lead in the desired direction.

When I met with Dianne, I was surprised to find her quite assertive in challenging my perceptions that without a reinforced wake-up call from me, her shop was not going to make it. She reviewed the history of her coffee shop, and offered me a vivid sense of what she and her longstanding colleagues had accomplished over the years. It became clear that although the shop epitomized an affable and genuinely warm atmosphere to all who crossed its threshold, this was not just some passive alignment between a group of 1960s-era, laid-back folk and a coffee shop. Beyond this natural fit, Dianne and her coworkers reliably and purposefully made the necessary effort to assure their business was unique and satisfying in a predictable and sustaining way. Dianne was straightforward in communicating to me that it was only this past year that the expectations had shifted to profit. She elaborated that although financial data and marketing plans were of course useful, they are about action. In many of their discussions in recent months, she and her coworkers had conceptualized how to build up from their rich and valued work culture and business to one that made money, too. She had cut out articles from *The Wall Street Journal* for the staff to read that validated the ideas that Michelle and I had stressed about the industrialization of many services industries, including the coffee shop business. Basically, she was saying that she was working with them to prepare to make the necessary changes.

Struck with what I had missed in understanding the greater depth and complexity of Dianne's problem solving and communication to her staff, I nevertheless found myself impatient and worried that although well intentioned, she was moving too slowly. She was essentially betting on the staff's ability to "get it". Since moving into this job, I had discovered the existence of another category of human being—different from energetic sales types like myself—who basically couldn't understand business realities. Therefore, you had to tell them what to do. I could do that and, notwithstanding Dianne's comments, that is what I planned.

At that point, I noticed an almost imperceptible nonverbal indication of irritation on Dianne's face. However, if it was there, it passed quickly. She told me that she was glad I planned to come to the shop and actually thought it would help all of us. However, she was firm in asking that I not give a formal presentation. As an alternative she offered to have the staff meet with me in small groups. There would be 16 people at the shop for the monthly meeting. Dianne said she would accompany me in sitting down with groups of four for an hour each. I thought it was a nuisance to give my speech four times, but not wanting to seem overly controlling, I went along with her recommendation.

Dianne met me at the door on the day of the scheduled visit. She escorted me to one of several meeting rooms to which we have access through our rental arrangement with the building landlord. Given the stakes of ultimately winning or losing based on the outcome of this visit, I was moderately anxious, but I felt no lack of confidence with regard to the validity of what I had to communicate. My discomfort lay in not being exactly sure how to enforce the right balance of seriousness and threat to move this group off what appeared to be dead center.

Before I had an opportunity to launch into my comments, one of the staff offered me the communal bowl of popcorn. I knew that I was not there to eat popcorn with the gang; on the other hand I did not want to come off negative and rejecting so I accepted it, grabbed a handful, and started chewing. Meanwhile, Dianne set the stage, explaining that I was there as a follow-up to my last presentation about the need to shift more into a business mode so we could realize a profit. Surprisingly, she then asked the group of four what, if anything, they wanted to pass on to me in the way of thoughts and perceptions. At this point, I felt a very strong need to introject and make it clear that I was not there to get a progress report or update because there had been no progress. There was a new "sheriff" in town and that was me. But again I did not want to appear domineering, so I allowed for what I thought would be a brief and isolated comment from the group. However, more to the point, my throat was suddenly very dry, littered as it was with popcorn, and all I could do was squeak out a request for water. I was told that there wasn't any, but that they would get me some soon.

While I remained unable to speak, one of the staff launched into her concerns that moving into a business orientation would allow her no time to bring coffee to her customers' tables and visit with them. She saw this as a likely loss to their warm, friendly culture. Another staff member validated this as a legitimate concern, yet wondered, given that they were considering reduced staffing across extended hours, if by necessity some of this personal contact would have to be reduced in order to cover the most basic of responsibilities. He also noted that free refills were a distinguishing feature of the shop, and suggested that a fresh pot be made available at regular intervals in an accessible area.

At this point, another worker communicated with considerable energy that Roberto's was no longer the only coffee shop in their old part of the city, but was now one of three. One featured French coffee, whereas the other carried the name of the city and was often associated with sport events and civic activities upon which the community's image had been built. Her concern was that neither Michelle nor I were moving the business agenda along quickly enough. This woman had worked for Dianne for several years while attending a nearby college. Roberto's provided her with enough income and benefits to cover her expenses in a bare-minimum fashion. Her concern and motivation was that should Roberto's fail, her security was at risk. In response, one of the most senior workers stated, with quiet authority, that the long-standing clientele would stand by them through the necessary adjustments. However, he made the point that they needed to be very attentive to maintaining that part of their core identity that was customer based, so that they could retain as many of their customers as possible.

Meanwhile, I was dying with fragments of popcorn lodged in my windpipe and I had developed a form of transient laryngitis. Before I knew it, 4 hours had passed and I have been moved from group to group through the room with more polite, earnest requests that I join them in eating popcorn. Thankfully, before I left the last group, I had been granted a glass of water and regained my lost voice.

In the parking lot, Dianne thanked me for caring enough to come and meet with the staff. She told me that it was clear I had had a very successful encounter with the workers, and that it was obvious that I respected and understood the struggle they were experiencing in this necessary transition. Most important, she told me, was that I listened rather than lectured. That told them that I was confident that they could figure out what they needed to do within the parameters and timelines I had set.

As I drove back to the office, I had a few thoughts. The first was that not since boot camp at Fort Benning, Georgia, during a sweltering July, had a glass of water tasted so good. Second, I understood what Woody Allen meant when he said that 70% of all success is showing up. Finally, I was surprised that Dianne and her staff were addressing the issue of the transition. My surprise took two forms. First, I had not known that was going on. Second, I was puzzled that they didn't just make the necessary adjustments and stop the pondering and preparing.

The Rest of the Story

Okay, so let me tell you the rest of the story as the situation unfolded over the next 6 months. As this store had a history of success, although that success was defined somewhat differently in the past, it became successful again within terms that defined success in the present. It did take longer than many of the other stores to make the necessary changes. However, Dianne and company had been able to stretch to and maintain their positive gains. Although they employed many variations of their basic strategy, they collectively wrote a letter to their customers explaining in everyday language that the coffee industry had changed and that they too needed to change in order to prosper as a business. Customers were given the letter in an envelope when they came into the store. Some of the more familiar clientele actually received an envelope with their name on it. Dianne and the staff communicated in the letter what they considered their fundamental strengths as a coffee shop (which wouldn't change), and then they identified the additional products they would be promoting and services that could be offered, such as catering for work gatherings. They asked their customers how close to the mark they were in proceeding as outlined, and requested feedback about what additional things they might do to strengthen their relationship, based on good coffee and a relaxing atmosphere. Dianne had already agreed to implement the top three recommendations, prioritized by the work group, provided they did not result in significantly greater expense or go against the company's policy or core mission.

The long story made short is that a desirable financial trend became obvious in 3 months, and black was seen on the profit-and-loss chart for the first time 3 months later. At that time, Roberto's, under Dianne Spark's leadership, regularly sponsored book club meetings; in addition, a handful of local businesses used its services to provide coffee and pastries at their functions. Also customers occasionally mentioned that they had come in that day for coffee at Roberto's, rather than the competition, because they valued the shop and didn't want to lose it in a market shakeout.

QUESTIONS ABOUT THE BEHAVIORAL ASPECTS OF LEADERSHIP

So there you have The Popcorn Chronicles, illustrative of leadership challenges we have encountered ourselves and observed among many others. Although there are a number of ways you might evaluate this case study, we have selected a set of questions to consider about the personality and behavioral aspects of leadership.

We begin with a very broad question. Is it helpful for you to separate out leadership versus management behaviors of any of the principals (Joe, Dianne, & Michelle) of the case study? One view is that managers carry out responsibilities, exercise authority, and focus on getting things done. Another perspective is that leaders are concerned with understanding people's beliefs and gaining their commitment. In other words, some would argue managers and leaders are different in what they attend to and how they think, work, and interact. Although the leader–manager debate has generated tremendous controversy, there is not much to support the notion that certain people can be classified as leaders rather than managers or that managers cannot adopt behaviors required of leaders for success. We maintain that it is important for all managers to think of themselves as leaders, and consequently we use the term *leadership* to encompass leadership and management behavior. What's your take on this?

First

As you begin to put these managerial and leadership behaviors into the job of taking charge, what is the first order of business? It appears that the starting point is to determine *what* needs to be accomplished, which is often more straightforward than *how* are you going to go about it. *How* speaks to thinking about engagement of the impacted people: how to evaluate the dynamic and changing environment in the industry; how prepared you are for this particular piece of work. Success in this effort is not simply something that can be predicted based on how bright a person is. On the average, leaders have already passed the brightness test. That's why they were selected for this assignment. More to the point, then, is how open and broad is the leader's psychological style of taking in a lot of information and comparing and contrasting what's known and what is needed to be known, to achieve the desired end in this specific situation.

Joe has well-established access to a set of ideas and actions that have guaranteed success for him in the past. He also has enough flexibility (and humility) in his style to know that the Regional Vice President role may not be an optimal match-up with his natural strengths. Dianne, on the other hand, is masterful in organizing information about people's experience; what makes for an inviting, aesthetically pleasing environment; how to navigate conceptually across a range of value systems. She registers Joe and Michelle's sense of urgency and immediacy. At the same time, she has a strong sense of the staff's concerns about losing both a work environment that is part of their well-being and possibly losing their employment if they don't make the necessary adjustments.

In a general sense, what we observe in the case study is the information system part of the leadership equation. That is, the "making sense of a situation." It is obviously a very individualized process as evidenced in Joe's and Dianne's styles. Given that the integration of their conceptual orientations is stronger than either alone, the lingering question is how can we use these individual and collective personality characteristics to the maximum advantage in our leadership work?

Second

So you are a manager and a leader and need to figure things out. Once you have the picture in focus, what's next? As you know, any idea, even a richly informed and accurate one is nothing without action. Good ideas are a dime a dozen. The most observable aspect of leadership is purposeful action.

We see this in detail with Joe and Dianne. Each in his or her own way and with an individual sense of timing has moved out into the world communicating a particular message of what needs to be done. With Joe, the message is intensely urgent. He doesn't want to be perceived as negative, yet it is clear in his mind that if he doesn't become assertive and, even if needed, aggressive, all will be lost by virtue of not gaining enough targeted action. Dianne's activity is stylistically different. She gets out front with her coworkers and leads them in working the issues. The ultimate strategic action is important to her, yet it is secondary to having the confidence that the work group has enough understanding to make its problem solving something other than a surface, and potentially fleeting, engagement.

This behavioral characteristic of leadership carries with it a recognition that the extraversion portion of the personality operates on a continuum both between passivity and activity and between being warm and outgoing to being reclusive and restrained. You can see that both Joe and Dianne have shown a scattering of strengths and limitations if not weaknesses in their leadership behavior. Joe's sense of "do something now" is realistic and relevant; Dianne's social engagement is both necessary and wise. Yet separately, their personality-based problem-solving styles have the potential of being lopsided in this situation. Again within the constraints of who we are as people, can we expand our strengths, get tuned up where we are under-powered, or partner with others whose style gives us more balance?

Third

Consider social engagement for a moment. How do people determine whether the contact leaders have with them has depth or is primarily just a mechanical part of the job? The character of social engagement is largely about whether workers perceive that the boss is concerned about their welfare. Can you trust this man or woman? Does he or she give you straight information that holds up over time? Are there any apparent higher ideals that seem to bring life to the leader's behavior other than the bottom line, control, and prestige?

These questions are easy to state, but the complexity of measuring people against them is another matter. Although many of us might say that we would like Dianne to be our friend, and that we don't know about this Joe guy with his transparent need for power and expectation of compliance from others, the larger reality may not be so simple. Without Joe calling attention to the need to re-evaluate how the business is run, complacency could reign and all would be the worst for it. On balance, if we had to consider only Joe's orientation, it may be very hard to look around the corner to see his enlightened direction. His sense of alarm gets in the way, obscuring any confidence that he may have in his workers' ability to develop adaptive solutions. His approach implies that the worker simply needs to row harder and longer in the industrial slave ship. Productivity gets main billing without much consideration of work culture and reasonable personal needs.

This personality–leadership characteristic is as much a matter of the heart as it is of the mind. Leaders who oversympathize with workers' difficulties in making changes can become paralyzed. Those who view this problem dryly as an abstraction of common sense miss the true nature of people and how to motivate them to make needed adaptations. Leaders who register only the value of the business are heartless robots, whereas those who consider only the worker's needs are sentimental fools. Is this an either–or proposition, or do most leaders show some individualized variation on this dynamic? Can you learn from your personality style to balance this leadership characteristic?

Fourth

Already it is clear that taking into account the need to be both a manager and a leader, to figure things out, to be active and social with a balanced consideration between people's needs and getting the job done, you have to question why anyone would want these jobs. In a word, being a leader can be stressful! We have all observed the range of emotionality that colors leaders' styles. Some leaders keep an eye to the horizon, ensure their colleagues are informed, and make the necessary adjustments without much angst. Others set off the cry of alarm, feel intense pressure to resolve the discomfort in the moment, and seem preoccupied with issues of wining and losing.

Leadership includes a multitude of wins and losses and the work environment is a constant interplay of staying the same and changing. How stressful is all of this? It depends on the individual. With regard to Dianne, it is helpful to recall that she hung in with the Old Town Coffee transition to Roberto's. Rather than avoiding this challenge, she was the primary person who carried the culture from the past to the present. After all that culture was the bedrock on which Michelle wanted to build her new company. However, we don't see much vigilant anxiety from Dianne, other than what was externally introduced. She subsequently followed up with her group concerning matters of profit and competition. Although external vigilance may not be her responsibility as a local manager, it does show the utility of having both Joe and Michelle in the picture. On the other hand, Joe's anxieties and his irritability that lies not far from the surface depreciatively distorts his view of others. Furthermore he is vulnerable to being considered driven by fear rather than opportunity. Yet if he could include more consideration for others in his approach to this opportunity, he would be seen as a leader with integrity, attempting to achieve a common good.

Of interest to all leaders is the extent to which they are controlled by their emotional needs as opposed to the preferred option of being informed by them. Registering concern about being out of synch with the marketplace can be enormously useful in making needed organizational adjustments. Without the ability to check into this worrisome threshold of human experience, corrective adaptations would be impossible. The important distinction to be made here is between how you feel and how you behave. Feeling anxious, vulnerable, discouraged, or irritable is quite different from behaving in those ways. How much emotionality can be controlled? How much do you want to control your emotion expression in your leadership capacity?

Fifth

So what remains? One more personality–leadership element is needed to make this process complete, and that is following through. No matter how "on target" we are with any of these elements, if we don't conscientiously and deliberately go about the business of achieving the desired end, we achieve nothing. To lead well over time, you must develop the discipline to create some form of order that guides you through a set of steps from start to finish.

We observe Joe and Dianne going through their own forms of due diligence. For Joe, this meant putting together the historical financial reports and targeting the market strategy to close the gap between the current and desired level of profit. When he saw a shortfall in Dianne's performance, he followed up with her (however flawed in his approach), and by dint of especially dry popcorn, listened and was perceived as supportive of his colleagues. Dianne's process was less linear, but no less crucial to their eventual success.

Once Dianne registered within herself the need to act, she engaged her coworkers to give them the opportunity to move to where she was headed with comprehension and readiness. Whether mapped out in her head or intuitively inferred, she knew that although the transition was led by her and Joe, their goals would only be achieved with and through the workers: Her follow-through was incorporating input from the customers concerning how to set their new direction. Once that was established, then the financial charting offered by Joe was helpful as the workers tracked their progress.

In the dynamic interaction of leadership behaviors, conscientiousness occupies a unique role operating as both a quiet motor that keeps the process running and the glue that holds the other parts together. It doesn't integrate the parts like the first element of being open to your experience does, but it does represent deliberation in keeping all the balls in the air to get the job done. As a stand-alone characteristic of leadership effectiveness, conscientiousness is singularly Spartan. Again, without it, nothing gets done. What does this mean if you are gifted in one of the other leadership behaviors, but conscientiousness doesn't come naturally to you?

CONCLUDING COMMENTS

As a note of closure, this chapter has included a familiar story of leadership in our times. In its own way, The Popcorn Chronicles is as heroic a fable as those of yore. There are protagonists who are our heroes and heroines; there are goals and worthy causes; there are personal flaws and real dangers; there are adventures! The heroes and heroines bring their strengths and struggles—the elements of their personalities—to ambiguous situations that are complex. We have identified the range of personality elements and the questions they raise. A point we could all agree on would be that, like Joe or Dianne, none of us have a perfect alignment between our personality and our leadership role. All of us must make the necessary adaptations. The 2nd Language of Leadership is a strategy to expedite that adaptation. As you will read, it is a way of learning effective leadership behaviors that would have been helpful to Joe and Dianne and to the rest of us as well.

Personality: An Organizing Role in How Leaders Succeed and Fail

Synopsis

This chapter provides a basic understanding of how an individual's personal style is connected to leadership effectiveness. We first define *effective leadership* as making sense of situations and motivating teams to successful performance. The fact that so many fail at these endeavors underlies our main premise that personalities that don't usefully correlate with the demands of the job sink more leaders than lack of technical skills. With the introduction of the Big 5 theory of personality, a "match-up" is made between the responsibilities of leadership and the role of personality.

LEADERSHIP DEFINED

Over the years, leadership has been defined in numerous ways. However, our goal is to simplify this complexity and to offer a definition that is commonsensical and accessible. One of our reference points is the scholarly writing of Robert Hogan from the University of Tulsa, who has done some original thinking and writing on the interactive relationship between personality and leadership effectiveness.

THE ROLE OF PERSONALITY

Among the questions that Hogan addressed are the following: Can you recognize good leadership when you see it? Can you predict who will be effective as a leader? Most people believe they can. To many, effective leadership is based on financial wizardry and oriented to a positive "bottom line." Although there is no doubt that good financial performance over time is an indicator of competence, those of us who have been involved in "start-up" and "transitional" ventures, know that the bottom line in a budget can be affected by situational variables outside of one's control. Sometimes, it is inevitable that you will lose money before you make it, even when all the factors of effective leadership are present.

So effective leadership isn't primarily bottom-line performance. Maybe it means being held in high esteem by senior leadership. In the minds of aspiring leaders, this is often given great weight. What could be a stronger validation than having an established leader say to you (as no doubt they have), you have got what it takes; without question you are made of the "right stuff"? That is not only validating, but it can be intoxicating as well. However, neither of these measures is any more reliable than trying to predict successful leadership based on an individual's height or hair color.

What makes leadership difficult to predict? First, you need a reasonable definition of leadership. We believe that the best measure of leadership must flow from the most cogent definition. Our view is that leadership is fundamentally a social influence process that culminates in reaching mutual goals with the leader's constituents. It involves making sense of a situation, determining the team's objectives, motivating people to work together to accomplish these objectives, and influencing team culture. In reality, leadership is not linear because there are no leaders without followers, and a leader won't be successful unless there is substantial collaboration and coordination with team members.

Most of the traditional leadership research has concentrated on the leader's influence on followers. Followers are often motivated to do more than originally expected because of their feelings of trust, admiration, loyalty, and respect for the leader. This motivation occurs when the leader assists subordinates in becoming more aware of the importance of the task and the value of the outcomes, under conditions when he or she provides an environment that will inspire and motivate them to overcome obstacles; it helps them think beyond their own self-interest to the needs of the work group and the organization. From this concept of leading, including making sense of the situation and using team-motivating behaviors, the most enduring and resilient indicators as to whether or not an individual is a good leader is the extent which he or she is perceived as such by the team members. Although this benign perception doesn't in itself assure success, reaching mutual goals without it is very unlikely.

Our definition of leadership may make the responsibilities of a leader appear deceptively simple. The fact is, they are not simple. Successful leadership is both an art and a science, and as such it is enormously complex. Far more individuals who are assigned leadership roles fail than succeed.

Let's attempt to sharpen our appreciation of the successful behavior pattern of the leader by exploring what the leader needs to do right. Workers characterize successful leaders with one word that represents their front-line experience. That one word is *integrity* and it incorporates well-intentioned, effective, and reliable behavior. Furthermore, when individuals are asked to cascade this description into 1,000 descriptive words, the results take a form very consistent with the Big 5 theory of personality.

The emerging question is whether the Big 5, as a proxy for personality, might serve as a useful and practical reference for leadership effectiveness. Again, we see leadership effectiveness as interchangeably "integrity" and "making sense of situations and motivating others to accomplish work," while recognizing that the former is the virtuous version of the latter. Read on and in the next section you can be the judge.

LEADERSHIP EFFECTIVENESS AND THE BIG 5

As a frame of reference, the definition of *leadership effectiveness* as making sense of a situation and motivating others to complete objectives serves as the backdrop to this discussion. Next, we articulate the Big 5 interpreted consistently with leadership effectiveness. In chapter 3 we review the Big 5 as a personality theory with implications of using it to plan behavior change in the form of increased leadership effectiveness. For the moment, suffice is to say that a great strength of the Big 5 factors is that each factor is substantially discrete from the others, permitting us to consider each as an important and distinct aspect of personality and leadership.

Openness

The first of the Big 5 factors is *Openness*, which includes elements of what we commonly describe as imagination, intellect, and openness to experience. This can be conceptualized as the ability to draw information both from within you and by scanning the environment to create the data base to "make sense" of, understand, or otherwise convert the situation before you into a cogent impression and a practical direction. In the Popcorn Chronicles, direction meant Joe's understanding the urgency to adapt to the new business environment, and Dianne's sense that getting her coworkers ready for change was the principal issue.

Openness is the information-system aspect of the leadership effectiveness equation, and it fits with the concept of understanding the continuities (or lack thereof) of experience from the past to the present. This means you are able to transfer from your previous experience the problem-solving strength that will give you an expanded understanding in your new situation. It also means discerning which unarticulated and unanswered questions prior experience has not prepared you to factor into your problem solving.

Extraversion

The second Big 5 factor is *Extraversion*. Within the context of leadership effectiveness, this means going to the world with a "sense-making" vision, mission, or plan and engaging others in implementation of activities. Extraversion is about having confidence in yourself and your ideas, and engaging the world with your leadership agenda in a friendly, but committed and passionate fashion. Mintzberg's thoughts and extensive writings about the well-rounded manager are consistent with this active, interpersonally connected construct of extraversion.

In the Popcorn Chronicles, we can examine the degree to which Joe demonstrated Extraversion. Joe's successes at Roberto's, first as a product line manager and then as a regional vice president, provided a foundation of confidence in himself and his ideas. Yet, one of the lessons he had not learned was how to engage others (namely Dianne and her employees) in the implementation of activities.

Agreeableness

The third Big 5 factor is *Agreeableness* which is more congruent with what we mean by nuturance and supportiveness. More than being easy to be with, this factor is the aspect of leadership that includes considering the needs and welfare of the employees who work for you. Leadership is about winning the hearts and minds of the workforce. To accomplish that, you need to know what is in their hearts, what is on their minds, and what they need and value.

In The Popcorn Chronicles, we can examine Joe's demonstrated Extraversion as an active, assertive leader. Alternatively, Dianne Sparks shows the positive, warm side of Extraversion. She demonstrates supportive and nurturing personality characteristics, is attentive to employees, and considers the security needs as well as the value and meaning of the work itself. She appears to understand employees and customers whose social needs are of primary importance. All of these are elements of the Agreeableness factor.

On the other hand, Joe takes a different approach. He talks about "being single-mindedly driven to achieve my stated goals. I believe in high quality products and excellent customer service, yet unlike Dianne, no one ever accused me of being warm and relaxed." Joe expresses concern for the security of the workers more as a byproduct and afterthought to completing the necessary tasks.

Although all the elements of leadership effectiveness are important, there can be no high-performance organization if you don't deal well with the Agreeableness factor.

Neuroticism (Adaptiveness)

The fourth factor is *Neuroticism*. Don't let the term scare you. Consider that the Big 5 was developed in an environment where the primary end users for the concept were mental health clinicians, hence the decision to represent one end of the continuum of this factor. We are deliberately choosing to use the other end of the continuum—*Adaptiveness*—which would have a high negative correlation with Neuroticism. For the purposes of studying leadership effectiveness, Adaptiveness means not getting caught up in unpleasant emotionality.

Adaptiveness is the ability to manage the complexity of the work world with a desirable level of comfort. It means a confident, but real presence. In other words, whereas Adaptiveness relates a nonanxious engagement, being "real" means that in the face of losses, the leader expresses sadness; in response to significant challenges, concern is demonstrated yet balanced with optimism and a viable plan.

In The Popcorn Chronicles, Joe feels overanxious about fear of failure. Alternatively, Dianne on her own may not be anxious enough to anticipate and make necessary adjustments.

Adaptiveness also goes beyond managing today's complexity, and speaks to a level of hardiness in identifying, responding to, and being innovative in the face of emerging and anticipated challenges.

Conscientiousness

Finally, the fifth factor is *Conscientiousness*. Specific to leadership effectiveness, Conscientiousness can be considered as either the glue that holds all the leadership activity together or as the motor that keeps the efforts going. We are talking about the self-discipline to follow through, the drive to develop the necessary competencies, the order and organization that assist cogent action, and the pursuit to reach the desired outcome. Without the other four factors, there is no content or direction. Without Conscientiousness, there is no accomplishment.

Again, as we refer back chapter 1, we see Joe's tenaciousness in making sure the staff gets the message and follows through. Dianne is diligent in assuring that needed action is preceded by winning the hearts and minds of her coworkers and customers.

CAVEATS AND QUESTIONS

As a dynamic interconnected set of characteristics, the Big 5 approach appears to have promise as a way to organize thinking about leadership effectiveness. For a typical overachiever who might read this book, some comments are in order. The first is a version of "buyer beware." Anything as complex and dynamic as leadership effectiveness won't ever be neatly packaged in a fashion that approximates absolute truth. As a prudent reader, you would be wise to think long and hard about buying this way of thinking until you do a critical assessment of sorting out how this works for you. Also, at this point, we are only introducing you to a way of thinking. Not yet addressed, and probably of more interest to you, is how you convert this approach into actions. This is addressed in later chapters.

By way of foreshadowing chapter 4 with the brief history on the Big 5, don't be concerned about how to perform at the 100% level on each of the five factors. It is not in the cards! You can no more study exhaustively to acquire a perfect IQ than you can achieve a perfect personality or its leadership-effectiveness equivalent. Like IQ, personality is largely genetically driven. Also it is important to consider that, depending on the leadership situation, what is needed personality-wise may vary. As you can attest, not every leadership situation will find an open, outgoing, considerate, unflappable, highly disciplined approach useful. The challenge here is to make the best of your unique personality configuration of strengths and weaknesses as it relates to the situation in which you choose to lead.

To further stimulate the skeptic in all of you, you are undoubtedly asking yourself whether this personality view of desirable human performance (here most specifically leadership effectiveness) had a life before Hogan organized his thinking. The answer is yes. Using concepts of four to five major traits as explanatory vehicles for understanding behavior have a long history. As we discuss later, the ancient Greeks played around with this idea long ago.

By 1948 Stogdill extracted information from previous research and developed five clusters of personality correlates with leadership, including capacity, achievement, responsibility, sociability, and popularity. The trait and behavior approach to leadership effectiveness enjoyed popularity prior to the 1960s. Subsequently, consideration of greater complexity within a strong empirical foundation has been incorporated within the Five Factor Model. As a technical reference point, when we discuss descriptive strengths of this school of thought, it is called the Big 5; when referring to its predictive abilities, it is called the Five Factor Model. For purposes of simplicity, we use the term *Big 5* interchangeably to refer to both.

The point to be made is that whether it is the 1950s or now, an effort to clarify a complex matter like leadership effectiveness is very difficult. Accordingly, a tension ranges from being too specific to being too general as we discuss and try to understand what we mean by leadership effectiveness.

How does this relate to the Big 5? We have presented a brief review of the thinking about leadership in relationship to the Big 5. However, for further exploration and examination of leadership research, numerous references of studies and writings from researchers and leadership experts that detail both the specificity and lack of interconnectedness of leadership findings may be found in the References.

The conceptualization could be criticized for being too general. One way to follow up on this criticism is to consider the Hypothetical Construct school of leadership effectiveness, which says that general approaches to leadership are too diffuse. The diffuseness results from the operating premise that leadership effectiveness is too abstract a concept to define specifically. Ironically, the Hypothetical Construct form of inquiry converges with another set of leadership effectiveness schools called Empirical, Implicit, and Emergent leadership.

The Empirical methodology includes asking for observations about well-established effective leaders and inventorying the behaviors that are believed to have made them effective leaders. The Implicit strategy breaks away from a focus on any particular leader. Here people are asked to identify "off the top of their heads" characteristics considered to be important for effective leaders. Finally, Emergent studies examine recently assigned leaders and identify those who are considered successful and why. Notice how all three research streams return us to the inquiry of describing effective leaders that in turn results in the Big 5 classification of leadership characteristics.

More broadly, a criticism of the particular link we are establishing with leadership and personality within the Big 5 is that it is too narrow as a set of explanatory constructs. Essentially, isn't personality more encompassing than the Big 5? What about the role that the character, value, and intelligence play in personality? It is easy to see that, relative to the range of what is included in personality, the Big 5 conceptualization is limited. It is also elemental. In other words, we have called out most, yet clearly not all, of the available building blocks in the foundation of personality that can be reasonably tied to leadership.

Also in consideration of the 2nd Language approach and its limitations, it is worth asking how character (what Cloninger calls "the acquired form of personality") impacts leadership. Both character and Daniel Goleman's concept of "emotional intelligence" are higher level constructs (with bigger and more complex behaviors) than the Big 5 elements. The strength of the 2nd Language approach is that it starts with addressing each person's unique personality. The weakness of the Big 5 and therefore the 2nd Language is that it is not comprehensive as a personality approach (on the other hand, what is?). It stabilizes personality into a handful of things.

On balance, the 2nd Language model is designed to assist you to build—most often for most people and situations—the behavior patterns that will work for you in the leadership role. As you will note we have represented the relationship between leadership, personality, and psychiatric problems later and separately in the book as the 3rd Language of leadership. Finally, it is worth emphasizing that this approach, like all approaches, is limited in its scope, applicability, and underlying research foundation. Hopefully you are both skeptical and open to its possible merits.

As a transitional note, we still need more study in the arena of understanding the problem of how to be successful as a leader. Therefore, the next section explores why so many leaders are unsuccessful.

WHY LEADERS ARE UNSUCCESSFUL

We believe that many leaders are unsuccessful primarily because of the lack of preparation and training in the necessary behaviors to achieve competence in functioning effectively. Without specialized training, individuals become discouraged with incomplete or inadequate leadership strategies. Rarely do leaders know or have the opportunity to acquire effectiveness skills congruent with the manner in which they best learn. In addition, little or no time is devoted to practicing key leadership skills except on the job. Let's explore these issues in more detail.

1. With rare exception, most of us enter leadership situations with limited preparation. Frequently, the lack of preparation is substantial, and although our skills in our professional craft may be well honed, the movement from craftsperson to leader is fraught with difficult transitions. Paradoxically, temporary adaptation to the leadership role is fleeting and illusionary because circumstances cause the requirements and expectations of the job to change.

2. Most children don't need special education to tailor the acquisition of basic skills into some form of knowledge base. The more complex the learning assignment, such as functioning as a leader, however, the more we value coaching that is oriented and personalized around our strengths and weaknesses. In any event, a complete absence of training seems very ill advised in an activity with high stakes that is as complicated as leadership. However, that is where it stands for most of us who become leaders. You go to school from 2 to 12 years to learn your craft-related skills. As for leadership, all that may be required is to show up one day and say you are willing to give it a shot.

3. The resilience of human beings notwithstanding, people in general, and leaders in particular abhor life situations that require constant coping.

Not surprisingly, many emergent leaders experience their initial outings into leadership work as exercises in coping. To the extent those early experiences don't evolve into a set of learned leadership skills congruent with successful performance, new leaders leave their roles in droves, often with no intention of returning. Given the value on control and accomplishment associated with leadership, moving out of the coping mode and into mastery is very important. Organizationally, either in the work world, or in the world of education, we do very little to assist this objective. It is reasonable to assume that there have been many instances of where failure in leadership could have been avoided had there been a meaningful, personalized program to assist new leaders in moving from a coping to mastery position.

4. The leadership effectiveness elements of making sense of situations and motivating people brings us to question how we do this. Basically, in leadership effectiveness, we are talking about working with events (situations) and people (team members). The lens with which we interpret this fundamental aspect of life (events and people) is our personality plus all of our accumulated experience and cognitive aptitudes that go with it. None of us is in a constant, accurate 20:20 focus through that lens. We all are in and out of focus, relative to any number of situational and static factors. We maximize, minimize, omit, and otherwise distort our experience to some lesser or greater extent. Given how important accurate reading of events and people are to leadership work, it is surprising but true that this is typically not an aspect of what has been described as necessary but quite limited preparation for becoming a leader.

What is available in the way of personality assessment is too often not helpful. Clinical personality tests like the Minnesota Multiphasic Personality Inventory (MMPI) are designed to identify psychopathology and tend to label subjects as unqualified for leadership. The question they often address and answer is, simply, "Does the candidate fit or not fit?"

Personality measures like the Myers-Briggs have no strong scientific basis and tend to over-objectify people. This is limiting in itself and further compounded by validity issues. These measures are often not reliable over time, in consistently measuring whatever ambiguous behavioral dimension they purport to measure. Finally, there are a number of respectable leadership indices (SYMLOG, PROFILOR, BENCHMARKS). Their strength lies in picking up relevant aspects of leadership; their weakness is a failure to address the uniqueness of the individual personality.

Big 5 personality measures appear to be the best option, given this need for clarity about the role of self in the leadership equation and given the limits of the other measures. But again, we will discuss this later and you can judge for yourself. The point is that we have precious little to offer people that is accessible and affordable about the personality–leadership connection. Yet, this is absolutely a key to leadership success and failure.

5. Finally, let's consider psychological counseling as a reference point for determining whether people, including leaders, can be assisted in making meaningful change. Only during the last 20 years have we been able to say definitively whether counseling is effective; we do know that people are better able to sustain the gains from counseling if they are allowed to exercise initiative and draw from their strengths in developing and applying a problem-solving strategy.

This contrasts the prescriptive approach with counseling, where the helper imposes a direction from the perspective of the helper's view of behavior and change. We won't belabor what common sense tells us, that a course of support and information from others is good. Yet the most powerful and sustained learning specifically results from our own industry. Such self-efficacy draws from our history of strength and recognition of our needs. This is posed as an ideal for learning, whether it is for leadership effectiveness or fly fishing. What we have for leadership training falls far short of this. You would think that we would employ more of our most preferred training approaches in proportion to the importance of the activity. Curiously, we see little to no training that affords leaders to learn effectiveness in a highly focused, personally tailored fashion.

It is important to consider the significance of how accessible leaders are in recognizing and understanding their personalities. This is a variation of the JoHari Window of what others know about me, but I don't know about myself. It is appealing to think that leaders are less prone than other people to over-editing a positive picture of themselves. Little evidence supports that assumption, and some research actually suggests the contrary. Managers and leaders do not focus as accurately on their own personalities as other people do. It is also probably true that feedback from coworkers and others who provide input for annual performance evaluations tends to be positive. An important condition of being able to use information about our personalities includes the ability to know oneself and a willingness to use the information. This issue is explored in chapter 6 on Leadership Development Strategies.

It is no surprise that so many leaders fail. Actually, it is surprising that the few succeed. Leaders come unprepared and typically don't get specialized training. They become discouraged with a coping approach, are often not aware of their distortions, and usually have no idea about how to acquire effectiveness congruent with their preferred learning style.

Our argument is that those who succeed find that the equivalent of the types of preparations we have just described is typically absent. The concern is that the preparation is not intentional from the outset. Our intent is to provide you with the opportunity to organize yourself systematically with all five of these issues (preparing, training, moving toward mastery, reducing distortions, promoting self-efficacy) in mind for the challenge of becoming a leader.

CLOSING COMMENTS

Becoming an effective leader is a complex matter and very little is done to train and prepare individuals. It is not surprising that many leaders either fail or prematurely abandon leadership roles.

By now, we suspect, in addition to maintaining a healthy skepticism for what has been said, we hope you are also experiencing a good deal of curiosity about the topic of personality. Questions might emerge regarding the degree of flexibility and stability in personality structure, the historical and scientific background of the Big 5, and the meaning your personality might have for you as a leader? The following chapters explore all these matters and more.

Personality Fundamentals and the Big 5 Concept

Synopsis

We have a dual focus in this chapter. First, we briefly explore the fundamental question regarding the extent to which an individual's personality characteristics change. This question is relevant for the individual leader who has personality features that both enhance and impair leading. The answer is that adult personality traits in general don't change much. However, a spectrum of behavior that is realistic within a personality trait does offer a variety of options for a leader who must adapt to a particular situation.

The discussion of change is a prelude to exploring the Big 5 concept, the second emphasis of the chapter. Among the many theories of personality, the Big 5 has great utility. So what is the Big 5? How does it fit into the classification of personality theories? How is it best measured? What might your personality profile look like using the Big 5? Why is it important in understanding leadership effectiveness?

PERSONALITY CHANGE AND LEADERSHIP EFFECTIVENESS

To what extent can individual personality characteristics change? The primary emphasis is addressed in the context of leadership and the relationship between personality and leadership effectiveness. If personality stabilizes in early adult life, do we still have room to select from a number of ways of functioning that support leadership effectiveness?

In some overzealous drive to be an effective leader, many individuals are on a quest for a perfect personality. Does it really make any sense—even in the desirable quest for leadership effectiveness—to change our personalities? We have taken some time to make the point that, in some basic way, all paths to leadership return to us and our personalities. As we speak of ourselves, we articulate who we are in words that essentially describe our personalities. We have cautioned you not to pursue a perfect personality! However, you most likely believe, and you are right to do so, that each of us has a range of potential outcomes that determine how effective a leader we might be. That effectiveness we speak of is nothing more than a set of behaviors. If that is equivalent to personality, aren't we talking about changing our personalities? The short answer to these questions is that we would be well advised *not* to tamper with the structure of our personalities.

Within a reasonable range, however, we have options concerning how we choose to behave. Both to clarify and to offer an empirical foundation for these thoughts, we review work done by researchers Costa and McCrae on the stability of personality over the course of time. To balance their findings, we also examine the theoretical work of McAdams, whose thoughts about levels of personality give us a useful basis on which to consider behavior change and leadership effectiveness.

Personality Stability

To what degree is personality stable or fixed? To what extent does personality change? These questions have inspired curiosity about the extent to which personality changes over the course of time, which has been the focus of two research psychologists from the Gerontology Research Center of the National Institute of Aging. In the area of the developmental psychology of adulthood, each stage of life presents different tasks to be completed. Although the task may vary with age, much of the scientific community has believed that personality was relatively stable.

This impression of stability was not universally embraced, and it was not until Costa and McCrae did their work that the question received a rigorous evaluation. They used a large representative group of American adults who served as research subjects and asked them to complete a Big 5 personality measure that they had devised, called the NEO–PI. In this acronym the first three letters stand for the initial letters of three of the five personality factors of the Big 5 (*Neuroticism, Extraversion, Openness*) and the last two letters (PI) represent the words personality inventory.

The test was administered on multiple occasions over the course of time. Also, individuals who had knowledge of the subjects were administered a version of the NEO–PI that was structured specifically for an observer to complete. These results clearly indicated that adult personality characteristics in general, as measured by the NEO–PI, did not change much after age 30.

We observe adolescents formulating an identity during their teen years. Within their circumstances of aptitude (what they are good at), of temperament (emotional modulation of their experience), and of opportunity (situational factors such as who is around them and what is happening in society), teenagers try on behaviors and sort out an identity that is congruent for them and their context. Assuming that this task is mastered acceptably, during the 20s a young adult would address the next big questions of life, such as who am I and what might I do?

Accordingly, by age 30 it seems reasonable that most people would have a relatively stable sense of who they are and would operate mostly from that personality structure. As you think about it, to do otherwise would be destabilizing. Imagine if a person used his or her personality as if it were a closet full of clothes that one might take off and on. Such behavior would be very confusing to the people who had become familiar with the person and it would be disconcerting for the individual.

From another perspective, when an individual is over 30, his or her personality consists of patterns of ways of being in the world that provide and organize a consistent and efficient life strategy. Personality expression is "who you are" and "what you are attempting to accomplish." Furthermore, in seeking to accomplish your goals in life, using your personality as the available set of tools is more like playing baseball with batting averages in the 40% range as the optimum performance level. This is contrasted with school experiences where the range of performance is typically 70% for those who are passing, with 100% attainable for some who desire to achieve. Real life and the use of your personality-based behaviors to solve any number of problems, including leadership challenges, are considerably more complex than school with its structure and artificial pass–fail experience.

So what are we saying? Is personality like the lottery? If you have developed a "winning" personality by age 30, are you on the side of the line that equals success? If not, then are you out of luck? Not exactly. Admittedly, the importance of those first 30 years is not to be minimized given their impact on how much the remaining course of life will go. Daniel Levinson, the late developmental psychologist from Yale, devoted much of his life work to clarifying the limits and the possibilities based on people's prior experiences of what is possible across the life span. Many of you know his two major works, *The Seasons of a Man's Life* and *The Seasons of a Woman's Life*. As Levinson's studies show, early developmental experience both expands and contracts what is possible for us in the future. However, neither developmental progress nor personality are completely responsible for life's outcomes, including our success as leaders.

Personality has its fluid dimension and, given the dynamic, changing nature of life, there is a more inclusive and flexible way to consider the interplay between leadership effectiveness and personality than to conclude that by the time you reach 30, nothing will change. To draw that type of conclusion would mean that adults stop learning and become stagnant after the age of 30. Obviously, this is a complex question that centers around the age-old debate about nature versus nurture in determining how people will behave and lead.

To include the factors that influence leadership behavior is to balance genetically fixed with environmentally flexible and adaptable aspects of personality. Costa and McCrae represent the fixed aspects. A recent study of how transformational leadership emerges as a shared focus of self-awareness across a subset of identical twins (vs. fraternal twins), concludes that leadership has a hereditary component. The thrust of this book is to acknowledge what is hard-wired in leaders' behavior patterns and then address the question of what can be modified and how.

LEVELS OF PERSONALITY

Dan McAdams, a leading expert on personality, sheds light on the question of what aspects of a leader's behavior can be modified so that we can move beyond a rigid sense that there is a stark dichotomy between winners and losers in the leadership effectiveness game depending upon where you land at age 30. McAdams conceptualized personality on three levels. At Level 1, we are talking about the relatively static factors of personality including our traits, inclinations, propensities, and the like. This refers to how our behavior patterns in general might be described. For example, *the leader was outgoing and optimistic*. He concurs with Costa and McCrae that by the time people are well into early adulthood this aspect of personality, represented as the characteristics we *have*, is well established.

Level 2 of personality are behaviors we emit or the things we *do*. This is the expression of our traits and personality inclinations into specific behaviors. For example, *the leader stayed for the whole meeting, during which she was actively engaged, expressing great confidence in the new initiative*. Given that Level 2 operates within the ceiling and floor set by Level 1, it covers a range of possibilities. That is, an introverted person is very unlikely to change into an outgoing, demonstrative people person. Nevertheless, a range of extraverted behaviors could be shown by this person that range from none to some. This individual may use these extraverted behaviors depending on any number of contingencies. The relevant question might be how important is it for things to go well in a particular leadership situation where extraverted behavior will have impact? Yes, the introverted leader can and probably needs to be extraverted in certain situations. On the other hand, it is unrealistic to expect him or her to change completely into an extravert.

TABLE 3.1

Levels of Personality

Level 1 *Traits*	Personality as who we are. This organizes relatively static factors of personality including our traits, inclinations, propensities.
Level 2 *Behaviors*	Personality as behaviors we emit or the things we do. The expression of our traits, personality, and inclinations into specific behaviors.
Level 3 *Life history/trajectory*	Personality conceptualized as the life we live that flows out of traits, circumstances (historical and present), behavior, and organizing values. Organizer all Level 1 traits and all Level 2 behaviors according to what is important to that person in his or her life situation.

Finally, we have Level 3 of personality conceptualized by McAdams as the life we live. Level 3 organizes all Level 1 traits and all Level 2 behaviors according to what is important to that person in his or her life situation. In this way, personality becomes the study of persons' lives, which flows out of their traits, their circumstance (historical and present), their behaviors and their organizing values. In summary, we have Level 1 personality = traits, Level 2 personality = behaviors, and Level 3 personality = life history/trajectory (see Table 3.1).

How can we apply McAdam's thoughts about personality to leadership effectiveness? It is important to note that although there is a relationship between leadership effectiveness and personality traits, there is no master leadership trait per se. On the other hand, there will always be a set of behaviors that will be more or less successful in making sense of a particular situation and motivating people to accomplish work. Those behaviors do of course relate to personality traits as interpreted within the Big 5 structure and it is the selection of specific behaviors within the structure of the Big 5 that signifies leadership effectiveness.

This does not equate to a mechanical process of ritually pursuing idealized formulas of leadership effectiveness associated with the Big 5. The question, "Can personality change?", becomes significantly more real when we register that there are behavioral expectations for a given situation that may or may not converge with our particular Big 5 configuration. Given the innate nature of how personality as a Level 1 phenomenon emerges, we may never have a comfort level with some of the behavioral expectations for certain leadership situations. That is, those Level 2 personality characteristics needed in a given situation may include expression of behaviors that are finely tuned and automatically either accessible or underdeveloped. Furthermore, we may be so limited in the necessary personality characteristics and behavioral expression that the rational choice is not to select that leadership assignment. The best we can expect of ourselves behavior-wise (Level 2) where we are underdeveloped or limited is an acquired (vs. natural), effortful (as opposed too relatively effortless) performance. In other words, a portion of our leadership behavior repertoire will always be like a "2nd Language."

This creates a ceiling and floor for varying aspects of leadership effectiveness. This range of behaviors results in achievable levels of leadership effectiveness that capture the interest of those who choose leadership as an important part of our lives.

Before exploring various aspects of the Big 5, we examine the classification of personality theories.

Classification of Personality Theories

Our perspective is that personality theories serve one major purpose and fall into three classifications. The major purpose is to make available a method of putting information together so that it is most serviceable. There is nothing messier than looking at uncoordinated information that is difficult to use and contains random and isolated pieces of data.

The three classifications of personality theories (illustrated in Table 3.2) that are not necessarily mutually exclusive, are the Empirical approaches, Psychological-Assessment approaches, and your own School-of-Thought approaches. The Empirical approaches involve the scientist conducting studies with the purpose of putting together a systematic body of knowledge. These approaches allow you to have confidence that a theory, among other things, describes accurately what it purports to and that it can make useful predictions or offer accurate descriptions on the basis of what

TABLE 3.2
Classification of Personality Theories

Empirical	Addresses scientific questions.
	Do adult personality characteristics/behavior patterns change?
Assessment	Address whether and/or how much of a personality characteristic a person demonstrates
	How open is a specific person to learning from his or her experience?
School of Thought	Addresses the effort to organize one's observations into a systematic model of behavior.
	Is there a relationship between childhood experience and adult adjustment?

it tells about people. Empirically, as with the Big 5, you may be studying a broad range of personality factors that includes virtually all or most human behaviors. On the other hand, you might be examining a narrow range of behaviors like the authoritarian personality.

The second classification, frequently related to the first, includes the Psychological-Assessment approaches. These models give you an idea about how particular sets of human behaviors are arranged according to certain constructs or patterns. The implied assumption here is that you want to evaluate whether or not people share enough characteristics in common to be members of a particular group. For example, in the most commonly used clinical personality test, the Minnesota Multiphasic Personality Inventory (MMPI), the questions asked (and accordingly the related constructs addressed) measure whether people coming for counseling are having problems with some type of distress, rigidity in personality style, or difficulty in sorting out reality from fantasy, or any combination of these.

Finally, School-of-Thought approaches, based, for example, on Freud, Jung, and B.F. Skinner, who weave sets of experiences such as impressions, observations, or experiments into some cohesive fabric. The models that emerge are broader than the first types of theories based on scientific investigation and may or may not be particularly compatible with the relatively narrow use of theories for assessing individuals.

In summary, the first classification, represents a scientist interested in generating a system that accurately describes human behavior; the second classification includes the test makers who want to assess whether particular behavior patterns are present; and the third classification presents a model to organize the information that has been collected.

This takes us to the next set of questions about the Big 5. How does it fit into the classification of personality theories? How is it measured? These are the questions we review next.

WHAT IS THE BIG 5?

The Big 5 is a novel approach because it is consistent to some extent with all three classifications of personality as illustrated in Table 3.2. It is consistent with the empirical classification and is primarily free of any preconceived way of thinking about human behavior; it is like the assessment classification, to the extent that it can be used to assess people, although it was constructed more to describe people in general as opposed to categorizing them; it is less like the school-of-thought classification because the originators didn't begin with a system of thoughts before they had data.

The Big 5 flowed from the data, rather than its originators naming an approach and then looking for supportive evidence. The latter may be a subtle point. Our intent is to keep the theory in perspective from the vantage point of how it is experienced by the end user. Personality theory should not be someone's pet idea or a biased attempt to gather data to put an individual into a box with a codified set of numbers or letters. Whether it is a question of learning more about ourselves as effective leaders or responsible citizens, individuals want to be understood, not objectified.

HISTORY OF THE BIG 5

Dating back to ancient times, there was talk of possibly four or five dominant personality traits. However, in the past 20 years, two behavioral-health scientists, Lew Goldberg at the University of Oregon and John Digman at University of Hawaii conducted landmark work on the Big 5. As basic behavioral scientists, Goldberg and Digman were interested in developing a personality theory that was valid in describing people as a necessary first step toward enabling optimal prediction of behavior as a second step.

Goldberg and Digman's focus was the universe of adjectives we use in the English language to describe human behavior, and they questioned whether there were a limited number of categories (called *factors*) into which those adjectives fit. Although there is a long story of encyclopedic proportions about how the factors were derived and how their findings are similar and different from other leading scientists in personality, our interest is in leadership effectiveness rather than statistical analysis and the scientific discovery process.

Goldberg and Digman recognized that prediction is part of the scientific endeavor and encouraged other researchers studying personality and behavior to consider testing the Big 5 model. Their motive was to ensure that the future beyond their initial efforts would not be impeded. Goldberg and Digman were influential in encouraging two other behavioral scientists, Costa and McCrae to use the Big 5 factors in their "Does Personality Change Research?" From that effort, Costa and McCrae developed a method of measuring this with their instrument called the NEO–PI as we discussed earlier. They worked with the Big 5 approach in extending the research base from description to prediction. Costa and McCrae vary some from Goldberg and Digman on how to conceptualize the work to include Extraversion. Also, Costa and McCrae called their perspective the Five Factor Approach rather than the Big 5. At the risk of offending the originators, we simply refer to this collective work as the Big 5.

What matters is that the Big 5 is an easily applicable approach. It is helpful because it is a theory that relates to your life experiences. In other words, it is a familiar language. The very words we use in our everyday discourse to describe ourselves are the foundation terms in the Big 5.

To make this a serviceable model for you it is not necessary to learn the esoteric language of psychoanalysis and read all of Freud's original works. Using the five categories Costa and McCrae developed—*Openness to Experience, Extraversion, Neuroticism-Adjustment, Agreeableness*, and *Con-*

scientiousness—we don't need to go far beyond the brief description of each concept to use their factors to describe categories of behavior (or in our case leadership effectiveness) and make predictions about how and how well a person might perform in the future.

Let's look at a well-known leader, Ted Waitt, founder and CEO of Gateway, and use the Big 5 model to describe his behaviors. Waitt demonstrates his remarkable Openness to Experience through risk-taking behaviors, looks for new ways to capture opportunities in the environment, and operates with the concept that there are usually numerous ways to solve problems. For example, he acts as a role model for employees and continually demonstrates an interest in feedback; he meets on a regular basis in colloquiums that are open gatherings for employees and the public where participants can ask questions and offer new ideas; he empowers employees to make decisions without strict bureaucratic policies; he fosters visionary leadership.

We can also predict where the Openness to Experience characteristic might become evident in a range of future situations. Waitt, for example, loves the company colloquiums and the interaction with the audiences. He admits that this challenges him and prepares him to be creative. We can also predict how Openness to Experience might be perceived as, or actually be, a limitation or strength depending on how much it works off empathically building a consensus versus showing a lack of focus. Even worse, it could be an indication of performing a manipulative sham.

Before we talk more about individual traits, let's turn to how the Big 5 is measured. In the next section we discuss the use of the NEO–PI instrument and the Mini-Markers.

NEO–PI

Several years ago, an article published in the *Journal for Personality Assessment* included a critical review of all the Big 5 measures. The results of the assessment determined that of the half dozen instruments used to measure the Big 5, the strongest instrument was the NEO–PI. In brief and without going into further detail or proving statistical methodology, the NEO–PI was found to have the strongest validity and reliability. *Validity* relates to how well the test measures the characteristics it has been designed to assess. *Reliability* means there is consistency, and that the instrument measures the same thing, the same way, with approximately the same outcome over time. The higher the reliability and validity, the more accuracy for the assessment across individual and multiple administrations. The NEO–PI also received a strong endorsement in the 12th *Mental Measurement Year Book*, which is a report card of sorts for psychological tests.

The NEO–PI instrument consists of 225 questions. Each question requires a response based on a 5-point scale that measures the extent to which the behavior is or is not like you. Consistent with all we have said, the NEO–PI is only for adults and can only be acquired by individuals who have the required training in psychological testing. In other words, it needs to be administered and interpreted by a person who has the appropriate preparation to engage in the complex and sensitive process of translating the knowledge of statistics and test structure into the realm of interpersonal feedback and dialogue. The test is published by Psychological Assessment Resources in Odessa, Florida.

The description of the five domains is a generic version of what we discussed in chapter 2 when we framed the meaning in the context of leadership effectiveness. As a brief reference of Costa and McCrae's domain portrayals, consider that:

- *Openness* represents an active intellect, curious, imaginative, and independent in forming opinions.
- *Extraversion* reflects a socially outgoing style, being affable, optimistic, and assertive.
- *Adaptiveness* (Neuroticism) indicates people who are relatively free of distress in all forms, and who can take on complex and difficult situations while maintaining stability and balance.
- *Agreeableness* means that, separate from being the sociable extravert, this individual is altruistic and very considerate of the other person.
- *Conscientiousness* taps into self-control with the associated actions of planning, organizing, and following through.

As implied with Adaptiveness, all of these Big 5 domains are bipolar, meaning that the scores in each domain represent a level of being high or low in that major characteristic. As mentioned before, high or low scores don't necessarily predict that the associated behavior patterns will be most adaptive in specific leadership situations. Finally, each of the five domains have six subsets, called *facets*. The facets are more specific subsets of the particular Big 5 area. As illustrated in Table 3.3, *Self-discipline* and *Competence* are facets of Conscientiousness.

The NEO–PI is a controlled and copyrighted measure and therefore we cannot include it in this book. Notwithstanding, its use does represent the best available assessment of your Big 5 status, and it is important to have some idea about how this structure of the Big 5 applies to you. With that in mind, the next section of the chapter discusses an alternative to the NEO–PI instrument called the Mini-Markers.

Mini-Markers

Gerard Saucier, a psychology professor at the University of Oregon, came from the Goldberg and Digman school of the Big 5 and has done some useful research building off the original work of these two pioneers. Relevant

TABLE 3.3
NEO Personality Inventory—Revised: NEO PI–R

Domains	Facets	
Neuroticism (Adaptiveness)	Anxiety (Relaxation) Angry hostility (Serenity) Depression (Acceptance)	Self-consciousness (Personal comfort) Impulsiveness (Self-control) Vulnerability (Resilience)
Extraversion	Warmth Gregariousness Assertiveness	Activity Excitement seeking Positive emotions
Openness to experience	Fantasy Aesthetics Feelings	Actions Ideas Values
Agreeableness	Trust Straightforwardness Altruism	Compliance Modesty Tender-mindedness
Conscientiousness	Competence Order Dutifulness	Achievement striving Self-discipline Deliberation

Note. From Costa and McCrae (1992).

to this discussion, Saucier was impressed with how encompassing the Big 5 theory was as a way of describing the vast majority of human behavior–personality situations. He worked with Goldberg's 100-item adjective checklist that was designed to assess the Big 5 personality structure and explored whether it was possible to come up with a shorter and easier way to construct the measure.

Saucier developed a 40-item checklist known as the Mini-Markers. Although it has a sightly lower level of reliability than the original Goldberg measure, on balance, the Mini-Markers represents a positive trade-off with gains in efficiency (i.e., takes less time) while not adversely impacting validity. In other words, it provides a broad overview of what you can assume would approximate your Big 5 factors if you took the NEO–PI.

Shown in Fig. 3.1 is the 40-item Mini-Markers Set. Completing the test is self-explanatory. For each adjective, assign yourself a number between 1 and 9 according to the scale given. The number represents a range of how the specific adjective more or less represents what you are like. There are 40 items organized in five sets of eight items according to the appropriate Big 5 factors.

The Appendix includes a thorough start-to-finish example of the procedure for scoring your Mini-Markers so that you can be sure you have computed your scores correctly. This will also allow you to get an overall

	Inaccurate					Accurate		
Extremely	Very	Moderately	Slightly	Uncertain	Slightly	Moderately	Very	Extremely
1	2	3	4	5	6	7	8	9

	Column 1	Column 2	Column 3	Column 4
Row 1	____Talkative	____Extraverted	____Bold	____Energetic
Row 2	____Cold	____Rude	____Unsympathetic	____Harsh
Row 3	____Efficient	____Practical	____Systematic	____Organized
Row 4	____Moody	____Temperamental	____Jealous	____Fretful
Row 5	____Complex	____Creative	____Philosophical	____Imaginative
Row 6	____Withdrawn	____Shy	____Bashful	____Quiet
Row 7	____Kind	____Sympathetic	____Warm	____Cooperative
Row 8	____Sloppy	____Inefficient	____Careless	____Disorganized
Row 9	____Envious	____Touchy	____Unenvious	____Relaxed
Row 10	____Deep	____Intellectual	____Uncreative	____Unintellectual

FIG. 3.1. 40-item Mini-Marker instrument.

perspective as you record your score into a normal distribution profile of roughly what your percentage rank would be (where you stand high and low relative to a statistical model of comparing you with a mythical 100 other men or women).

Before closing here, we make a comment and offer a caveat. The comment is that you will notice in the appendix that Saucier takes the high road and uses the concept of Emotional Stability rather than Neuroticism. Also, he and his predecessors think in terms of not only Openness (to Experience) but also Intellect and Imagination. This conveys a more active cognitive process than represented with the NEO–PI where information is gathered, but not necessarily integrated.

The caveat is that what you obtain from this exercise with the Mini-Markers, while useful, is nonetheless a distant, mountain-top view of the Big 5 as it applies to you. As you will note in the subsequent chapters, the NEO–PI's facets, and particularly when they are high and low, play a very significant role in conceptualizing and strategizing how to improve leadership effectiveness. So the Mini-Markers is useful for exposure purposes, but it is not thorough or exact relative to you as a person who provides useful direction. The level of specificity that the NEO–PI provides in conjunction with the use of a fill-in-the-blanks questionnaire (see Appendix) that is specific to the 2nd Language strategy will become apparent in the examples included later in the book.

WHAT'S IMPORTANT ABOUT THE BIG 5 AND LEADERSHIP EFFECTIVENESS?

To know that there is an opportunity to choose among a set of personally congruent behaviors that increase the likelihood of functioning as an effective leader begs the question if we are not able to clarify more substance about the relevant personality theory. In this case, that is the Big 5. You have already reviewed the definition of leadership effectiveness and its relationship with the Big 5 in chapter 2. However, that level of information is not enough. To seriously evaluate whether you are going to begin to use this information for improving your leadership effectiveness, you will need to know more about the merits and strengths of the concepts presented in *The 2nd Language of Leadership*. Without the understanding, you are operating out of a vacuum without any solid foundation.

CONCLUDING COMMENTS

We have stated the case for using personality as an organizing concept in tying together the diverse knowledge we have about leadership effectiveness. The Big 5 theory is presented as having utility. Furthermore, it comes from the body of knowledge that also incorporates addressing the research issue of stability versus plasticity of personality traits over the course of life. Correspondingly, the outcome of that research that favors stability of Level 1 traits has also invited scholarly criticism that helps us understand the behavioral expression limits and possibilities of trait personality. You now know enough about the Big 5 history, its pioneers, and the principal test associated with it to make you completely familiar with this area of knowledge. You should feel comfortable knowing:

- The theory carries no agenda or bias of the originator other than to see a personality model embedded in the English language.
- There is a set of adjectives (or descriptors) that might be organized for us to accurately and reliably describe people and to anticipate their likely future behavior.
- The NEO–PI provides a valid and consistent picture of how people behave both in relationship to the five broad domains and relative to the specific subsets.
- The subsets, although not having the power of the Big 5 to pull together many related concepts, do alternately have the strength of specificity.

- Being high or low on the subsets indicates something very specific about you; this is less true with the generality of the domains (also called *factors*).
- The Mini-Markers gives you a thumbnail sample of how in a very rough way you might sort out according to the five factors.

You are in a position where you have heard the argument that personality is a viable contender for organizing and describing a complex behavior like leadership effectiveness; you have an idea about what is crystallized and malleable about personality (and therefore leadership effectiveness); you are well on your way to a solid sense of what the Big 5 is as both a theory and a method of personality assessment. Now it is time to put personality and leadership effectiveness back together so that we use the organizational and descriptive strength of these two concepts to develop strategies for improvement in effectiveness.

Chapter 4 focuses on how to think about this topic from the perspective of categories of effectiveness and on the area of greatest potential referred to as 2nd Language. Finally, we concentrate on how to use what we know to our greatest advantage, including leverage strategies, the good news about learning personal effectiveness, and goal setting.

Three Languages of Leadership

Synopsis

Leadership presents itself in varying levels of effectiveness. This chapter examines three different sets of personality–effectiveness interactions that leaders may demonstrate, which are identified as the three languages of leadership. The term *language of leadership* is used because, as a personality theory, the Big 5 derives from the English language and because leadership effectiveness tracks, in a literal sense, with the metaphors of a 1st and 2nd language.

For the 1st Language of Leadership, consider individuals working from their strengths and maximizing an alignment between personality and specific work needs. As a 2nd Language of Leadership challenge, suppose the individual is functioning well but nonetheless struggles with certain aspects of the job where the relationship between some personality factor and some key job requirements is not strong. Finally, consider the 3rd Language of Leadership. Imagine the individual performing poorly where an apparent mismatch exists between the person and role, or the individual is experiencing a period of difficult adjustment.

These three sets of circumstances all include the dominant relationship between leadership effectiveness and personality. The first has to do with strengths, the second focuses on managing weaknesses well, and the third deals with situations that are not currently matched to expressed personality characteristics. These three situations identify the 1st, 2nd, and 3rd Languages of Leadership, respectively.

PRELUDE TO LEADERSHIP'S THREE LANGUAGES

An obvious way to understand interrelationship between leadership effectiveness and personality is to think in terms of annual performance evaluations. Whether it is yours or one you complete for a subordinate, two essential questions are asked in these annual reviews: What does this person do well in the job? How can he or she improve? Ideally, feedback will be provided in response to both questions if improved performance is expected.

Within this context, you can broadly envision three outcomes—*outstanding*, *good*, *needs improvement*. These outcomes run parallel to the three languages of the leadership concept. Think about when you may have received or given such feedback. As you do this, the leadership language concept will become clearer as it becomes framed in your experience.

Sometimes the match between who we are and what was expected of us overlaps beautifully. These situations demonstrating congruence can be referred to as the 1st Language of Leadership. This congruence doesn't usually permeate our leadership experience completely. A more typical situation is the set of circumstances where there is an incomplete overlap between personality strengths or gifts and the challenges that the work environment requires. So, on the one hand, there is a place for a strong appreciation of our personality gifts. More often there is a broader world of situational demands for leadership juxtaposed against our personality limitations. Accordingly, we all struggle at times. Most individuals recognize these aspects of life and make the best of leadership situations. This brings us to the 2nd Language of Leadership.

The 2nd Language of Leadership is the part of our behavior that results from a struggling effort that may never become natural or automatic. We may always need to approach these situations of imperfect fit between our style and leadership circumstances with care and thought, and perhaps support and consultation. This effort differentiates the 2nd Language from the 1st Language.

Many leaders, even great ones, may experience some time of derailment. The challenges may be simply bumps in the road or an uncomfortable ride on a foreign highway. The extent of the derailments may be temporary or they may be disabling. This "off-the-track" scenario is what we refer to as the 3rd Language of Leadership.

Again, we believe the most important area is the 2nd Language of Leadership. Let's be realistic. Consider the situations where you have learned and grown the most. If you are honest, you will probably admit that your work life is a continuing struggle with strengths and weaknesses. On the other hand, it is where you have the greatest potential for development.

Correspondingly, in order to give the 2nd Language the emphasis it deserves, this chapter includes a review and clarification of each language, complete with examples. In chapters 5, 6, 7, and 8, we develop in more depth ways to think about and develop the 2nd Language.

1ST LANGUAGE

In this section the Power, Transformational, Paradigm Shift, and Social views of leadership effectiveness are summarized (see Table 4.1). First, we demonstrate the close relationship between the fundamental tenets of each of these leadership views and personality characteristics that converge with the Big 5. Examples of leaders who typify the view are described as they represent the 1st Language concept.

Power View

The Power view is characterized by the ability to face the world with a strong sense of mission and to accomplish what is necessary in a confident, clear, firm way. Any number of leaders may come to mind here, some more or less benign than others. For example, consider Norman Schwarzkopf, an Army general who was swept into public consciousness with the Persian Gulf war. Or think about a notable former First Lady, Eleanor Roosevelt. The 1st Language strengths that have become almost synonymous with these two publicly acclaimed individuals are obviously courage (high Adaptiveness), commitment to achievement (high Conscientiousness), and certainly optimism and assertiveness (high Extraversion). Both of these individuals had the fortitude to speak out and challenge the complacent. They put their mission ahead of their image, and they knew how to use the press to shape public opinion.

The fact is that most leaders to whom we give the highest praise will be viewed positively across the Big 5 spectrums. However, the Power school candidate will be especially high in Extraversion.

TABLE 4.1
Four Views of Leadership

Power View	Transformational View	Paradigm Shift View	Social View
Strong sense of mission; confidence	Accomplish what is possible; articulate ideals and vision	Look for new order; Entrepreneurial	Ability to lead with care; concern for employees
Extraversion dominates	Openness to Experience dominates	Openness/Conscientiousness dominates	Agreeableness dominates
Eleanor Roosevelt Norman Schwarzkopf	Martin Luther King Leslie Wexner	Bill Gates Martha Graham	Mary Kay Ash Howard Schultz

Transformational View

The Transformational view focuses on leaders who have idealized influence, inspirational motivation, intellectual stimulation, and individualized consideration. The leader constructs a culture that is dedicated to and supports a creative and empowering vision. An example of a leader who fits the Transformational view is Martin Luther King, Jr.

Martin Luther King, Jr. looked beyond the racism and prejudice in the United States and articulated a dream of racial equality. His dream continues today to draw a society toward a very desirable ideal. This type of leadership, emerging out of a personal conviction, galvanized a generation and has continued to contribute to gradual progress, amidst often grim and discouraging events.

A leader who is more flamboyant than Martin Luther King, Jr., while still exemplifying this view, is Leslie Wexner of The Limited, Inc. Wexner converted his vision of a nationwide chain of women's sportswear stores into a reality through his own hard work. He stimulates employee participation in discussions and decisions, challenges his workers by frequently raising the standards, and encourages employees to share his vision of the company's future.

Arguments could be made for any number of the Big 5 traits as dominant factors that make up the 1st Language. These individuals possess Openness (to Experience), with Agreeableness coming in as a close second. What emerges center stage is the openness to see what is obvious and possible. It is through this sort of open leadership that the rest of us are able to see and experience the highest levels of human performance.

Paradigm Shift View

The Paradigm Shift view has an element similar to the Transformational view but also includes scanning the environment for new opportunities, as well as taking risks about new ways of doing things and conducting business. The Paradigm Shift view moves beyond what is possible in the current realm of things and looks for an entirely new order, taking on an entrepreneurial focus. In the most basic way, the Paradigm Shift view is about a change in basic assumptions. A noteworthy example of this school is Bill Gates. Gates looked at the emerging world of information technology and saw a significant opportunity in the development of software. With puns intended, Gates opened up a new window through which information could be made available, that actually has transformed how we function on a daily basis. From the perspective of a 1st Language, he also would be a candidate for Openness with Conscientiousness included, given his workaholic style.

Alternately to Gates, consider other Paradigm Shift leaders like Pablo Picasso in transitioning us from standard realism in art to his geometric representations, or Martha Graham with her liberalizing dance from traditional formulas into the lyrical flight of movement she inspired.

Social View

As a key feature, the Social view focuses on a leader's ability to lead with a truly caring and benign view of others. This leadership approach looks for ways to enhance employees' job satisfaction and organizational goals. For example, Howard Schultz, CEO of Starbucks, is considered a "visionary with values." He demonstrates self-respect for employees and focuses on helping others strive for success, making a difference and contribution to the community, and rewarding workers for courage, integrity, and social vision in business.

Another leader who exemplifies the Social view is Mary Kay Ash, an entrepreneur who started her own company, Mary Kay Cosmetics, almost 40 years ago. Although this direct sales company has changed over the years, Ash's organization is still governed by rules that focus on fundamental core beliefs. People are more important than the plan; make them feel important, praise them, reward and respect them, and instill a sense of pride and pleasure to help them to do their best.

Both Schultz and Ash demonstrate a talent for being able to empathically understand and value the positive nature of individuals. Certainly, leaders in this category express great strength in Agreeableness as a dominant 1st Language of Leadership.

With these views of leadership effectiveness and the various examples of leader behaviors, the objective is to dramatize something universal rather than to suggest that the 1st Language of Leadership is reserved for the leadership gods. All of us in positions of leadership have benefitted greatly from our 1st Language strengths. However, on a personal level for the well-known leaders as well as ourselves, no one has strengths across the board that will serve well in every leadership contingency. We all experience demands for which our response ranges from halting and uneven to acquired yet never fully automatic 2nd Language.

2ND LANGUAGE OF LEADERSHIP

Before you finish this book, you will have read many examples of the 2nd Language. In the next section, we provide examples drawn from ways that the first author became interested in this notion of leadership languages out of his own direct experience. In what follows, we have Mike tell his story in his own words.

MIKE'S STORY

My standard, highly predictable greatest strength has been Conscientiousness; I have a long history of behaving in highly disciplined, generally well-ordered ways where I develop the necessary competencies, keep focused, and usually achieve my goals. Sound very boring? On balance, it has not been boring or even that easy because of my Achilles heel in at least one aspect of the other four factors.

In everyday experiences this means, conscientiousness strengths aside, there are a variety of situations that I find difficult. I will give you several examples and you can begin to see the facets of the NEO–PI surface that are challenging. These are the situations that make leadership frequently a 2nd Language exercise.

A Case of Being Surprised

The first case represents a situation where I was surprised. The example does not refer to any actual person, but it is true about me. The situation has repeated itself across time, and fortunately my 2nd Language adaptation has been such that I am not surprised as often. When I am surprised, I can recover more quickly.

Many years ago, in one of my previous leadership roles, a colleague working for me had a wonderful idea about an innovative program. Even better was the fact that some available discretionary funding was earmarked for this type of project. This colleague was a highly creative person who, although able to articulate a vision of a very richly developed program, was not very disciplined or able to get people and activities coordinated to make things happen. On the other hand, I was often constrained in my own ability to be creative by too often overemphasizing the practical problems that could interfere with my consideration of various possibilities. So, we were in some respects a good match.

To complicate matters, in order to receive funding for this program, my first step was to present the proposal and to receive approval from senior leadership. While I was in the process of delivering my presentation to the senior leaders, my creative colleague interrupted me. I was so intently focused on communicating the proposal that the interruption surprised me, and I was displeased to have a break in my flow of thoughts. In retrospect, it was not very realistic for me to think this individual would just sit by passively during my presentation. He is a fountain of ideas and it would be somewhere between naive and inattentive for me to think that he would not interject his comments at any point when they might occur to him.

Unfortunately, I was not paying much attention to him, so although I told him (after I counted to three to keep from showing my irritation) to please hold his comments until I was done (along with mentioning that this entire proposal was his "brain child" and that when I finished, his thoughts would be not only welcome but also desired), he interrupted me again. Foolish me! During the stress of the presentation, I mistakenly thought that my limit setting would have some sort of magical effect that actually had never been observed previously with my talkative coworker. However, having been distracted from my more typical alertness concerning his typical behavior, I was off balance, and my anxiety quickly transferred into anger. In fact, I was annoyed enough that I lost focus and I had certainly lost my poise. I was very fortunate that a third person who had worked with me in the clinic completed the presentation.

The rest of the story is that we received approval to request the money, it was awarded to us, we did good things with it, and I believe we all derived real satisfaction from the work. The point of the story is to demonstrate how my personality characteristics got in the way of my effectiveness that day. Within the Adaptiveness factor, I have a low threshold for Anxiety (Adaptiveness facet) and when stressed over time or surprised, I can become frustrated and Serenity challenged (also an Adaptiveness facet). I have since improved my ability to realistically anticipate the impact of demand situations like the one mentioned. I have also become more centered around the realization that if I want an anxiety-free, always-ordered universe, leadership is the wrong job. In other words, I need to expect a level of the unexpected. It makes no sense and is completely useless to rail angrily against events and people over which you have limited control. This is 2nd Language self-talk.

Call for Clarity and Direction

The next example relates to my current job, where I am the director of a mental health department in a Northwest HMO. I have been in the job for 10 years, and my first few years were especially challenging for me relative to 2nd Language struggles.

To put the situation in context, the director's role was a stretch for me both in responsibility and in the challenge of leadership during a time of considerable complexity and ambiguity. When the job was made available to me, I conferred with my family and advised them of the significant sacrifices that would be required of me (and us) to be successful in the role. With recognition that this job would limit free time at home, I received my wife and sons' support and took the job. Again, it was a time of significant transition where the objective was to find a new direction for the department, particularly in contributing to its success as a business. As I anticipated, this would often result in a 6-days-per-week effort. With support from my family, friends, and colleagues, I poured myself into the work and was successful.

In our organization, one of the strongest indicators of success is the annual performance evaluation input that is offered by those whom you lead and those with whom you collaborate to do the job. In any given year, 30 to 50 people contributed their thoughts about my progress through the annual performance evaluation process. Given the focus of this 2nd Language concept, it is amusing to think in retrospect about the nature of the input. Basically I heard that people were quite impressed with my work ethic and my commitment to mental health service delivery (a.k.a. Conscientiousness). Specific examples were offered about how this or that financial or organization goal was set and met. On the other hand, although the general tenor was that I was functioning at an excellent to outstanding level, questions were regularly raised such as "Where is Mike taking the department?", "What is his vision?", "What is the action plan?", and "Why don't we actually see much of Mike?"

I was pleased with the feedback about my strengths, but frankly, I was put off by the questioning comments. In my mind, I had worked hard to move the department in the very important directions of becoming better connected with the organization and the business community. In other words, I had not yet centered the reality that I alone am the director; that I am expected to give the job 100% effort; and that any shortcomings in my style and in my performance are up for comment and criticism.

I thought that I was doing so well with my strengths that somehow it was not fair to criticize me on my weaknesses. So, to be blunt, for several years, I discounted the questioning input as noise to ignore. It was only gradually that the feedback convinced me that the nature of this input was consistent over time. Also, the people offering the feedback were valued and trusted colleagues. I recall saying a little helplessly to my supervisors that I didn't know that I could do much about these questions because they addressed my personality characteristics, which don't change much.

Let me explain what I learned in NEO–PI language based on the discussion from chapter 3. Notwithstanding Conscientiousness strengths, although generally Open to Experience, I was relatively less open in terms of Actions (facet of Openness) by way of identifying specific plans; while fine in the Agreeableness area, I was relatively more indirect in my communication, showing less Straightforwardness (facet of Agreeableness); I demonstrated Assertiveness (facet of Extraversion) about what was important to me, and although outgoing enough to do my job, I am not high in Gregariousness (also facet of Extraversion). With these personality features, combined with Adaptiveness inclinations to circumvent situations that cause me anxiety, it is a small wonder that I would have these questions asked of me.

Need for Action

These two examples represented a need for me to take action to develop a 2nd Language that was more effective in my leadership role. There is something to be said for being honest about not knowing the best way to think about a leadership situation, the associated action steps that are needed, or the strategic direction of a situation. However, employees need leaders who regularly offer a clear vision of where they are going, why, and how they are going about doing it. This opens leaders' thinking to challenge. Staff members don't follow a direction if they don't understand it or have an opportunity to work it through. Again this doesn't mean that the leader blindly and naively communicates everything that he or she is thinking. It does mean that, at a minimum, leaders start with impressions and build a consensus with team members or at least allow themselves to be influenced by input.

In a leadership role, it is important to be specific and straightforward about desired strategic directions. It is also important to be available to the staff to allow enough of the necessary discussions that are the essence of determining whether they will allow you to lead them. You can always manage the staff, but for the more substantial business of winning their hearts and souls, the staff decides if we may lead. Finally, these situational challenges are not offered to suggest that leaders can structurally change their personality simply because of circumstances. However, this doesn't preclude you from being situationally aware of the need to modify some facet of your personality for leadership purposes.

These two examples show that although 1st Language strengths may get us into the leadership job, it is only as we begin to develop greater access to ourselves and 2nd Language learning that we determine whether we will stay with leadership and succeed in it. Also for many of us, the stress of being in the leadership role has led to or will lead to a 3rd Language experience, which is discussed in the next section.

3RD LANGUAGE

Our intent in this section is to make the point that the leadership journey is not always smooth. We may refer to these periods of time metaphorically as blow outs, train wrecks, derailments, or, in a more psychiatrically oriented style, we can talk about the dark side of charisma where personality disorders lurk. We firmly believe the vast majority of leadership efforts are based on a concept that fundamental goodness can prevail and problems can be resolved and corrected. There are always exceptions, including individuals such as Adolf Hitler, Jim Jones, and Josef Stalin and their ilk, who did not have some overriding good in their value system that balanced their darkness.

In a later chapter, the 3rd Language of Leadership is discussed in more detail, specifically about how it relates to the average person in the work world. In this section, the interest is in conveying the concept of a 3rd Language. The essence of the 3rd Language is that the leadership behavior is not functional. It is more than a struggle. The two examples we present are the developmental adjustments of Steven Jobs, cofounder of Apple Computer, and the disagreeableness of Richard Nixon.

With both Jobs and Nixon, we have seen periods of defeat that parallel their personality limitation. We also observe the flexibility within their personalities to be aware of and make (or not) the necessary adjustments.

Developmental Adjustment of Steven Jobs

What ultimately mattered about Steven Jobs wasn't that he almost single-handedly created the personal computer industry, overturning what looked like an invulnerable establishment in the process, but that he took it all personally. Although it became fair game to question Jobs' quirky decisions and his offbeat behavior, no one ever doubted how he felt about what he was doing.

Jobs dropped out of college to build toys for people like himself and computer hobbyists for whom the dream of having a computer was every bit as gripping as owning a Ferrari. In 1976 he cofounded Apple Computer, Inc., and became a legend as much for the success of the Macintosh computer as for his leadership style.

Stories of his petulance as a boss at Apple still abound. In the early years, he was considered an egotistical micromanager who needed to control every aspect of the product. You see evidence of the Jobs' 3rd Language behavior as people talk about his odd self-indulgences and explain that he was both loved and feared. For example, every product needed to be an impeccable reflection of his own tastes: What good is it to have your own business if you can't use it to express yourself? It made sense that Jobs, insanely rich and merely 30, was banished from his own creation in a 1985 coup of Apple. He went on to start NeXt Corporation and also to purchase and run Pixar Animation Studios.

From this illustration, we can describe Jobs as high in Extraversion, especially in Gregariousness, and very assertive about what he wanted. He was direct and Straightforward in his communication. For example, he was just as likely to criticize as to praise. Much of his leadership during the early years at Apple demonstrated low Adaptiveness, especially Impulsivity and Hostility, when he couldn't identify with perspectives that did not follow his thinking or accomodate his opinion. Nonetheless, a conscientious persistence describes his leadership.

After more than two decades Jobs discovered that to be a successful leader, he had to experience a dysfunctional style and learn from it. He has not repeated the early mistakes and friends, competitors, and even former foes agree that Jobs has wrung out what we would call 3rd Language behaviors. He asks people for advice and actually listens. He has learned from his mistakes.

For a business leader, a highly idiosyncratic and egotistical form of openness and ad hoc decisiveness can over time be a deadly combination. However, with the other side of this broad Openness and this warm, outgoing, confident Extraversion comes the ability to learn from his experience. This learning was evidenced in his improved understanding of the leadership situation. He demonstrated a related shift in direction and the ability to convince others to accompany him when he left Apple to start NeXt Corporation.

Contrast Jobs' behavior with our next example, Richard Nixon. He firmly stated he was not a crook but shortly thereafter left office attributing his downfall to an unresolvable conflict in Congress. It seemed obvious that the votes for impeachment reflected his complicity in the Watergate break-in.

Disagreeableness of Richard Nixon

In this example, Richard Nixon, while still in the realm of the really successful, showed less of an ability to go beyond his personality limitations and learn. The term "less" rather than "none" is used because, even after leaving the Presidency in disgrace, Nixon resurrected and reinvented himself as a knowledgeable senior statesman, with considerable experience in foreign affairs.

Nixon's elevation to great heights as a politician can be attributed to many factors, and not all are complimentary to him as a person. However, he was a person of extraordinary drive and resilience; he extrapolated from his aloneness, frustration, and inferiority by calling up a vision of a silent majority who wanted a better world; he contributed astuteness about how to think about and organize in dealing with the opposition; he demonstrated acumen with respect to foreign countries where our political relationships were conflict ridden; he possessed stealth, cunning, and ability to manipulate a no-nonsense position when opening up relations with China and handling relations with the Soviet Union.

Unfortunately, Nixon's tendency to operate from a position of considering the world in terms of "who is with you" and "who is against you" deteriorated in domestic affairs with his enemies list and the Watergate debacle. His blindness to the limited effectiveness of vilifying people in his own country was obvious in his audiotapes and other documentation that he assumed would serve as historical support to his greatness as a chief executive.

Although most of us may slip in and out of the 3rd Language, in Nixon's early tenure as the reelected President, 3rd Language behavior predominated and it cost him his job. Think of him as demonstrating a very narrow and self-fulfilling Openness (actually un-openness) compounded by a reactive (angry) emotional Adaptiveness. This is exemplified by his inability to view contenders and critics as anything other than one-dimensional enemies. By design and necessity, these challenges to oneself are a big part of political life.

CONCLUDING COMMENTS

We have covered a broad range of perspectives including more specifics on the three languages of leadership. The 1st Language examined four views of leadership effectiveness and provided examples of how individuals connect their strength with the Big 5. For the 2nd Language, a sample set of the struggles as a leader was discussed. The 3rd Language presented an analysis of two leadership derailments.

We have created a picture to show that we typically go into leadership positions because of our 1st Language strengths; we succeed and prevail by understanding and managing our 2nd Language challenge; for many of us there are periods where we are ineffective as leaders with 3rd Language derailment. Because the greatest opportunity for realistic success resides in the 2nd Language arena, the next chapter focuses on testing this concept against three of the characteristic ways in which we find ourselves engaged in leadership situations.

2nd Language Challenges

Synopsis

This chapter builds on the information in the previous chapter about the three languages and specifically addresses the 2nd Language. The intent is to raise your consciousness concerning the universality of 2nd Language consideration. To do this, 2nd Language scenarios are presented. The three scenarios illustrate the frequent paths into leadership: (a) I'm the leader because my coworkers like me (a popular leader); (b) I'm the leader because the bosses like me (a high achieving the leader); and (c) I'm the leader because I'm good at what I do (a technical or an expert leader). We also clarify that these "calls" to lead are not perfectly correlated with readiness for or personality alignment with specific leadership situations. This will prepare us for chapter 6, where we review 2nd Language strategies to include recommendations for leaders in these scenarios.

UNIVERSALITY OF 2ND LANGUAGE THINKING

Everyday discourse about leaders falls into a mix of comments that essentially relate to what we like and don't like. Allowing for idiosyncracies that may be more unique to the criticisms from very specific workers and their needs for certain types of leadership behavior, we are far enough into this discussion to have a working knowledge of what we need from our leaders in terms of receptiveness and responsiveness.

Gary Trudeau of the Doonesbury comic strip considered George Bush to be so "absent" and prone toward care taking that he was invisible in the strip. For Trudeau, Bush only showed evidence of being alive, active and struggling both with the complexity in the world and within himself through the presence of the unintegrated evil twin "Skippy Bush."

Trudeau represented his perceptions of Bush's predecessor, Ronald Reagan, and his superficiality with the persona of "Rap Master Ronnie," who became known only through MTV-type sound bytes. Trudeau's implications concerned whether Reagan deeply thought anything through or held the chief executive position as the equivalent of a character role in a B-grade movie.

Bill Clinton did not escape Trudeau's caricature as noted with the waffle icon. Here was a leader who considers everything and at times appears to be everywhere, all in the name of pleasing people and keeping his job. This tendency is long standing. You need only review Clinton's letter to the University of Arkansas ROTC commandant to see the masterly ability to communicate an expectation of being criticized while simultaneously and seamlessly vindicating himself of all serious wrongdoing concerning his evasion from military service.

You could examine any of these parodies of the presidents through any number of the Big 5 factor lenses. For example, the invisibility/evil twin, rap master, and waffle images all call up a certain amount of concern with the Straightforwardness and genuineness that you associate with the Agreeableness construct. With Bill Clinton and his overexposed personality, we see a man notable for his intellect, Openness, and Extraversion, yet even his supporters don't brag about his directness, Deliberateness, and Self-Control. In his personal life, he has been observed as reckless and then studiously evasive. These are 2nd Language areas where little learning has occurred, and yet had it, Clinton would have been embraced by most U.S. citizens as truly extraordinary rather than a brilliant, but very much flawed leader.

The focus in this chapter is on understanding more than behaving. In support of understanding, let's start with thinking about other people who are leaders before you begin to spend much time thinking about the 2nd Language and yourself. Those other people have already included a few famous individuals. Additional examples are intended to bring frequently occurring situations to your attention so that the 2nd Language concept will start to become obvious and familiar. We want to stress at this point that 2nd Language is evident and just a standard part of life. Nobody is perfect; everyone has strengths; understanding both strengths and weaknesses can be a point of growth toward higher levels of leadership effectiveness.

In the next section, scenarios are presented as brief reports using all the information and concepts that we have reviewed thus far. Here is the template. The leadership situation is described followed by a NEO–PI overview, personality description, and leadership behavior expression. The purpose is not to teach you the technical aspects of writing reports, but to reinforce the basic ideas so that you can evaluate this way of thinking. Each scenario is prefaced with overview comments that address the representativeness of the situation and what fundamentally is happening from a 2nd Language perspective.

Before developing strategies for leadership development, we first review some ways of framing and organizing personal information so that it is most likely to be acceptable and congruent to you. Strategy issues are outlined in chapter 6 for each scenario. Please keep in mind that the individuals we write about demonstrate characteristics that generalize well. Just substitute your industry and your environment to make the necessary modifications.

2ND LANGUAGE SCENARIOS

Popular Leader

Our first example is from a situation where the employees have an important say about whom their leaders will be. They may either elect or have significant influence in determining which leaders will be selected.

Studies have shown the influence of a leader who is able to connect with the wants and needs of the group in a way where it can be seen and felt. This is extremely important where individualized concern and commitment are demonstrated to specific persons or when individuals engage in fulfilling the needs of the group by words and actions. These circumstances provide experience in the very human dimension of trust, caring, selfless devotion, and so on. The dilemma arises because these types of Agreeableness features are not enough for an individual to survive and prosper as a leader. Nonetheless, this type of leadership is very endearing to workers and creates great loyalty. It is ironic that this type of circumstance may create two interrelated sets of problems (a) when the leader doesn't have enough aggregate Big 5 personality strength to do the job and performance suffers, and (b) when the first condition becomes compounded by workers making excuses for, and trying to protect, the leader.

This type of scenario can present itself with a full assortment of Big 5 characteristics where there are weaknesses and strengths outside of whatever may be considered the core strength. The specific example is one of real limitation, predominantly in Conscientiousness. However, the major weakness could be in Adaptiveness and/or Openness where other poor performance problems could unfold.

As a leader, if you have the good fortune of being popularly acclaimed, question what 2nd Language strengths are relatively weak as you seek to serve the employees. Also it is important to question what the workers might not know or understand that is occurring in the environment that could and perhaps will (regardless of what you do) negatively impact their security.

Many leaders may have difficulty with the gift of carrying the heart of their people when it is not balanced with a realism about their personality limitations vis-à-vis doing the job for followers. It is important to remember that the job lives in a context that may start with the employees, but then goes beyond them to the environment of the industry, the purchasers, and the end user or customers.

Specifically, what are the high performance requirements that, if not fully registered by the workers, will imperil both their adjustment on the job and their general security, and may limit as well the opportunity to pursue other employment options? In other words, to lead well, you need to be very clear and honest about business realities, and that may not come naturally to one who holds the ideals of humanitarianism as primary in importance.

This 2nd Language dilemma is frequently encountered by those new to leadership (where you will likely find idealism), and for those who come from professions dedicated to the welfare of others (i.e., the religious ministry, social service, local politics, education, and health care).

The NEO–PI overview in Scenario 1 pinpoints the struggle of a family doctor who has characteristics that both serve and interfere with the commitment to care for others as a leader, not only as a physician.

Scenario: A Popular Leader

Leadership Situation

A family doctor, recently elected as a medical center chief, describes the dilemma of having been chosen because of her easygoing style, while feeling quite challenged to manage the responsibilities of following through. Her apprehension is that of feeling overwhelmed. She is specifically concerned that she will "let people down." She asks for advice.

NEO–PI Summary. Her domain of Agreeableness is very high; dimension of Concern, Adaptiveness facet of Vulnerability is moderately high; and Conscientiousness facets of Order and Self-discipline are moderately low.

Personality Description. The dominance of her good will, compassion, and optimism can be negatively offset by a lack of both preparation and rigor in managing life responsibilities. When circumstances aggravate the balance between these tendencies, she remains poised, yet subjectively feels out of control, concerned that she has inadvertently imperiled the welfare of others.

Leadership Behavior Expression. Incorporation of a consistent, credible consideration of the common good contributes to the perception of charisma and accessibility in this naturally social leader. However, her altruism and well-being may become compromised when the expectations of others cause her to assume responsibilities that require a level of organization and personal management that is neither a preferred nor a well-established style for her.

High-Achieving Leader

Another scenario of a well-trodden path into leadership is where the individual, when observed by senior leadership, has created a favorable impression. Whereas many situations come to mind about how this might occur, there is often a cluster of circumstances that become organized around an eager, outgoing, poised, new and/or young person, who is seen as an especially fine asset to or prospect for the organization. He or she may be physically attractive and very personable. The chemistry with the senior leaders is so strong that there is a directive to move this person up as quickly as possible. Alternatively, such individuals (often referred to as "fast trackers") may be very accomplished in what they have achieved outside of the organization, and accordingly they are selected because they become associated with the realization of the hopes and ideals as an organization seeks to differentiate itself into the future.

In other words, you are a brilliant information systems specialist, marketing executive, technical innovator, financial wizard, brilliant long-range planner ... in XYZ corporation ... and, so the logic goes, you will perform as well or better in a more responsible management position with the company. On occasion, senior leadership may share a romanticized illusion that with this new, often young (and seldom broadly tested in this environment) person, we can realize all that we have hoped for ourselves. This again is an example of overfocusing on substantial, but nonetheless one-dimensional, 1st Language strengths.

The specific example demonstrates that notwithstanding a history of aggressive achievement and its accomplishments, those who hope to live and survive the full life of leadership need some other elements in their personality portfolio as well. Most leaders, especially new and young ones, will be expected to experience and succeed at a number of leadership roles in their career path. For those of you who have demonstrated high achievement early in your careers perhaps as assistants to CEOs or as vice presidents in a specific area, who are given lateral assignments, or who start local and are slated for a quick move up, you need to have a full tool kit packed. The fact is, you may not know how to use all the tools, yet knowing that they are necessary is the first step to continued success.

We all know of managers who are favored by senior leadership, but who are not valued by their local team. The example summarized here involves a person who, dating back to high-school sports and academics, has always excelled on the basis of his individual performance. He has consistently been able to do a limited number of things exceedingly well, to the point where he has been literally and figuratively a super star. Now responsible for a team, which is not high performing or motivationally structured like himself, his history of focus on achievement and on self collides with the need for attention to others and the mechanics of influencing gradual improvements. The 2nd Language struggles here are obvious.

Scenario: A High-Achieving Leader

Leadership Situation

An engineer, first promoted to an administrator role after completing an MBA, has now moved from an executive staff position to a front-line leadership role. He reports concern with the discontinuities between his assertive, goal-oriented style and that of the comparatively less enthusiastic technical staff. He requests consultation concerning the mismatch between his history of having been the "all star" and his new role of coach of a team.

NEO–PI Summary. The domain of Extraversion is very high; the dimension of Concern, the Agreeableness facets of Trust and Tender mindedness are moderately low.

Personality Description. A background characterized by high energy and tireless activity of getting the message out, taking charge, and making things happen are the mainline strengths of this "standout" professional engineer. However, the optimism that emanates from extraordinary efforts collides with the often-encountered modest motivation and limited task focus of subordinates. This contributes to a demeanor that signals disappointment and frustration to others.

Leadership Behavior Expression. Leadership for this young man is an active verb joined with adjectives like outgoing, self-confident, assertive, and distinctly visible. The immediate translation of these characteristic behaviors vis-à-vis a less-than-stellar work group is to get tough, establish rules, and enforce consequences. Not surprisingly, disillusionment sets in when administrative action is followed by decreases in performance and morale.

Expert Leader

Another common path into leadership is that of individuals who so excel at their craft and are esteemed by others, that there is an untested assumption that they would make a good leader and manager as well. Although it is safe to assume that it is advantageous for a leader of people with technical knowledge and expertise to be held in high regard for discipline knowledge, that in itself does not assure that the individual has the requisite strengths in other areas to function well within the broad concept of a leader. The individual may have a remarkable facility for comprehending and communicating the intricacies of the craft, be it computers, mechanical systems, medicine, architecture, and so on, but that does not mean that the individual is capable of putting into context the work within the industry, within the framework of what is motivating to people in a sustaining fashion.

This default assumption is very much in evidence when most of our technical preparations do not include a track for teaching the leadership and management of technical work. Too often leadership training is left almost exclusively to the precarious and potentially very expensive process of trial and error.

Also there may be aspects of certain professional preparations that don't generalize well into the leadership mode. For example, surgeons are people of action who use aggressive and invasive problem-solving approaches. Psychiatrists tend to be relatively passive, nonjudgmental, and reflective in comparison. Litigation attorneys, by the nature of their work, focus and structure blame, building cases for who is right and who is wrong. These are a few examples of how the style and pace of a discipline can demonstrate competence to a constituency for purposes of building credibility. However, it is a serious mistake to confuse the utility of that style and approach as appropriate in the leadership role, in any one-to-one fashion, assuming that if it fits the professional role it will also fit the leadership role.

Another way of thinking about the role of leadership for technical or expert leaders is to question the range within which the individual is likely to perform well as a leader. If performance requirements are beyond the individual's competency, will his or her leadership ability be viable and/or how much training needs to be accomplished? This would be another situation where asking this question is important, regardless of the direction in which the anser may take you. We emphasize this given the potential damage that occurs when we ask technical leaders to assume unreasonable responsibilities, without the opportunity for support and training or at least the informed option of saying "no" to the offer.

The next example presents a pharmacist who is very well adjusted and who has excelled as a local technical leader and manager. Part of her strength as a professional and as a leader over time, has been to recognize that she prefers and excels in very precise work situations. Within the arena of self-awareness, this rigidity of preferred work arrangements is a strength and not a weakness. As you read, this presents some unique challenges when the work environment surrounding the technical work changes substantially, and as a result, what has been an asset in terms of uncompromising adherence to a technical process may become a liability. In other words, the change of circumstance and the associated modification of responsibility can shift a person from 1st Language advantage to a 2nd Language challenge.

Scenario: A Technical/Expert Leader

Leadership Situation

A pharmacist reports that a promotion to a regional leadership role has been surprisingly challenging. Her technical and adaptable strengths, which were the source of her initial leadership assignments, seem out of proportion now in relation to emerging job requirements. The associated complexity includes incorporating interorganizational mergers and subcontracted external pharmacy firms into successful management of her leadership role. With a willingness to return to a full-time technical role, she asks for consultation concerning the relationship between her personality and the new leadership demands.

NEO–PI Summary. The domain of Neuroticism is very low (therefore high Adaptiveness); the domain of Conscientiousness is very high; Openness facets of Ideas and Actions are moderately low.

Personality Description. The wisdom of choosing a life structure is quickly noted in this knowledgeable professional's dedication to the craft of concrete expectations, notwithstanding the duration or complexity of the work. Ambiguous situations have been consciously avoided in pursuit of fulfillment and purpose with well-mapped-out, challenging tasks. The behavior of "staying the course with the tried and true" in what can be characterized as both narrow and arduous work has contributed to long-standing job satisfaction.

Leadership Behavior Expression. She expresses a first class and unflappable temperament combined with aptitude and discipline. These have been key to this technical leader's success in conducting and organizing the work of pharmacy management. Although these strengths are instrumental in leading with a credibility that resolve most knotty personnel problems, they don't allow for a sufficient preparation in a transformational and highly political environment. With this self-awareness, she is willing, following some reflection, to return to predominantly technical work.

CLOSING COMMENTS

You might begin to question the utility of this Big 5 as a means to leadership awareness because you have not been given a corresponding set of tools for bridging this consciousness raising into the realm of action and change. In other words, borrowing from what we know about disease prevention through education or personal change by insight counseling alone, information is a necessary but insufficient condition of desired behavior change. Hopefully then, you are asking yourself about what strategies and factors need to be in place to assist the increasingly sophisticated leader as student to become an action agent who is expanding and pushing the limits of learning.

The next chapter is designed to respond to these needs. You will learn about what helps in going beyond understanding this model and actually implementing it. You will find these aids to change as consistent with your own experience of times when you were best able to make needed changes in your life. Accordingly, the next chapter includes discussion of enabling philosophies that address the question of what points of view make it easier to change; clarification of strategies that address the question of what things, when I do them, most regularly result in desired change; and the integration of all of these into a template for bringing together situational data with personality data for the purpose of creating specific interventions meaningful to you as an individual. In chapter 6, all of this is summarized into a relatively simple conceptual schema that incorporates everything we have done so far. Furthermore, this conceptual schema is applied to the three examples in this chapter.

Leadership Development Strategies

Synopsis

This chapter provides you with enabling philosophies, effectiveness interventions, and a conceptual schema as you prepare to apply and implement 2nd Language information into useful actions. The enabling philosophies emphasize three principles: self-acceptance of the extent to which our personalities are relatively fixed, a related appreciation for the areas of great strength within our personality, and a realization that leadership behaviors can be augmented by the values we use to guide our lives.

    The effectiveness interventions include leveraging our weaker personality areas with stronger ones, partnering with others who complement us, and choosing to engage only in leadership work that realistically has potential for a desirable yield. Finally, the simple schema that the 2nd Language strategies rely on involve going through a sequence of evaluating several critical areas. Before doing anything else, the leadership situation must be evaluated. This is followed by an appraisal of our Big 5 traits, associated behaviors, and related leadership behaviors. After this sequence is completed, a strategy for increasing effectiveness can be evaluated.

    The enabling philosophies can put us in a behavior "change-friendly" state of mind, the interventions provide us with options, and the schema gives us a way to think through situations in a 2nd Language manner. To provide a more concrete and application-oriented framework, we review leadership development strategies for the scenarios that we presented in chapter 5.

PRELUDE TO CHANGE

Think back to leadership situations where you performed at your best. Now, think about some situations where you were less than effective and wish you had handled the leadership circumstances more competently. What differentiates the regretted performance from the preferred performance?

There is a set of factors that assist in optimizing our performance. We tend to perform competently in leadership situations (with our personal combination of strengths and weaknesses) when we have a "change-friendly" attitude. We behave competently when we consider options that are realistic, and use a way of thinking through the situation that begins with the current circumstance, takes personality into consideration, and then moves to strategies (2nd Language schema).

In the next section, we review enabling philosophies before examining effectiveness intervention options and the 2nd Language schema.

ENABLING PHILOSOPHIES

Effective leaders strive to perform at their peak levels amidst circumstances of complexity while drawing from areas of strength and weakness. These levels of performance most often occur when we are operating with several specific perspectives in mind that may be conscious and focused or implicit, brought to our attention after the fact. The point of emphasis is that there is no such thing as perpetual luck when you are in the leadership business. Either you assess how to view the world and yourself in a leadership role, or you will not remain a leader for long. The recommended perspective points include working from a high level of self-acceptance, where you recognize your strengths and acknowledge the values in your life as crucial in pursuing what is important.

Self-Acceptance

The first enabling philosophy of self-acceptance is the key to being able to move forward with a successful strategy. This point hinges on the underlying theme of this book, which is that no one has the perfect combination of behaviors and abilities to succeed as a leader in every situation. Individuals are incomplete, and becoming complete is not a simple acquisition process of going to the leadership skill store and buying off the shelf what you are missing as a leader. Wouldn't that make it easy?

Personality strengths missing from our leadership styles are primarily biologically grounded and have been further reinforced by life experiences.

For example, imagine that you are not endowed in the Openness domain with incorporating emotional information into your problem-solving behavior. Regardless of your personality, this is an important element of your job to either demonstrate or supply emotional leadership to your followers. It would be important to know at least two things: First, emotional leadership is important for you to succeed in the leadership role, and, second, that it does not come naturally for you.

The concept of self-acceptance is based in part on a belief system and in part on the results of scientific findings that you are fairly well fixed with your personality. The related implications are that we can deny, minimize, rage against, overemphasize, or accept those structural parts of our personality that are Level 1 (those that predetermine how we tend to behave) and are not going to change much. That is, we will always be swimming upstream with these behaviors and tendencies.

Most important to understand is that self-acceptance is constructive. Paradoxically, to become more effective in leadership, it is important to be able to say to yourself, "This is the way I am." Correspondingly, I neither want to lose energy by overemphasizing how to improve these personality aspects, nor have them inadvertently get in my way by ignoring them.

Let's use Bill Clinton as the example. Self-acceptance means being able to recognize the combination of his great comfort in moving freely through town forum discussions with his apparent abundant openness to everyone and everything. This, combined with his lack of a natural straightforwardness can, and has on occasion, resulted in harm to his credibility. For those who want a president to be focused on the vital few, town forum openness is distressing and disorienting. For those who believe they have spent their political capital to support Clinton's actual, preferred agenda, the town forum approach feels unfaithful.

The first thing we need to do to ensure a reliable level of success as leaders is to identify the situations in which we are comfortable and skillful and the circumstances in which we are relatively less competent. This acknowledgment offers a reasonable starting point from which leadership growth becomes possible. To be able to accept yourself, it is helpful to understand the reality that many aspects of your personality have been determined genetically so there is only a limited amount you can do to alter it.

The 2nd Language approach is about both how to develop awareness and how to apply the techniques of the 2nd Language approach to achieve self-acceptance. Awareness creates accessibility both to who you are and to what you can accomplish. It allows individuals like Bill Clinton to recognize that he needs to be open and very clear in the same communication.

First, self-awareness, also called psychological mindedness, is a trait that lies somewhere between strong and weak in any individual personality. The principle of the "rich get richer" and the "poor stay the same or get poorer" applies here. In other words, if you are reasonably self-aware, you can probably become more so; if not, it is less likely your awareness will increase.

Specifically, we are referring to the role that defense mechanisms play to keep us comfortable with our sense of self. If a person is quite unaware of his or her personality style, it is probably because it is uncomfortable to be so.

Self-awareness can be uncomfortable specifically with regard to the Neuroticism (Adaptiveness) factor. Although this domain and the associated facets have been framed in a positive perspective of Adaptiveness, it is often difficult for people to acknowledge painful emotional states of anxiety, depression, anger, vulnerability, and self-consciousness. One way to circumvent this concern is to drop Neuroticism from the Big 5 in considering personality and behavior patterns. However, this does not make much sense given the importance of the Neuroticism/Adaptiveness dimension in personality and leadership. Can we really think of Nixon's leadership without considering his struggles with trust and anger, or Jobs' leader style without his impulsivity and need to micromanage and control every detail?

The preferred way to handle this factor would be to keep Neuroticism/Adaptiveness in the equation, but not to include more of it in the leadership development discussion than the person would find comfortable. Obviously, the only way to ascertain psychological mindedness or self-awareness is through a face-to-face consultation. Computer-based assessments cannot both register this characteristic and know how to manage it directly.

Finally, some situational and individual variables increase the likelihood that a person will build self-awareness. On the situational side, if a leader is working in an environment where senior leaders model emotional openness and where the leader is afforded safe opportunities to learn about and consider the use of such information about self, that bodes well for self-awareness. This brings into play the whole concept of *mentoring* in organizations and the value this behavior has for everyone involved.

On the personal side, if the person's value system is activated by the leadership challenge, this can result in significant motivation to do whatever it takes to lead well. This again would increase self-awareness.

The intent of *The 2nd Language of Leadership* is to demystify and legitimize the role of all aspects of personality in leadership. Although that is a noble goal and achievable for many, the ability to use and expand awareness of self is in direct proportion to how much of it is in place at the start.

Acknowledge Strengths

The Big 5 concepts of leadership provide useful tools to identify your strengths with regard to leadership relationships. You learn to link the strength to effective behaviors as you understand the situation. For example, if your strength is Agreeableness, your ability to understand and value the needs of others is extraordinarily potent in promoting an atmosphere where people feel heard and cared for. That particular strength is not just an idea, an abstract notion derived from the thin air of speculating about personality. Instead it is a major part of what you have done each day of your leadership life that makes a crucial difference in being effective. It represents behavior that is predictable and the characteristic that prompts others to ask for your assistance.

Individuals with high Adaptiveness include the type of leader who can make sense of things without letting emotions distort meaning. On the other hand, we may select individuals with high Extraversion because they know how to go out to the world to sell an idea, operationalize a plan, and engage others with their optimism and confidence.

The focus of this second enabling philosophy is to acknowledge this strength for the gift it is to you and to others. Many have said that it was Bill Clinton's ability to be open to his experience and to learn from it that led to his reelection as the first Democrat president to serve two terms in more than 50 years. Because enough people believed he could see the world through the eyes of the average citizen with a range of traditional Democrat and Republican values, he received the necessary support in the 1996 election. Regardless of whether you like Clinton or believe in him, the point is that he was able to draw from his Openness strength to increase his leadership effectiveness in the top leadership role in the country. The implications apply to all of us. Our personality strengths are real assets and they should be neither taken for granted nor over- idealized.

All of the Big 5 characteristics come into play for the successful leader. However, there are one or two areas that will be the strongest and dominant. A question in the leadership situation is what can I learn through the lens of my greatest strength? From the previous chapter, it means that, through the lens of strong Agreeableness, popular leaders would evaluate how they best serve their people without letting them down because of limitations. Adaptive leaders would ask how to keep themselves and the organization in balance. Conscientious leaders would clarify how to assure the job gets done when aspects of "getting it done" do not occur spontaneously with their followers. For the extraverted "can-do" person, it is a question of how to be active and aggressive in the leadership pursuit while addressing the worker's needs effectively so that the effort really works.

The essence of this specific enabling philosophy is to honor this area of leadership strength and treat it with respect. This includes recognizing the flexibility and elasticity of this strength as well as understanding the limits. Finally, here is one of several places to perceive the areas of weakness within your own style so that you can begin to think about how to lend the strength of your most powerful domains for augmentation.

Role of Values

Values play an important role in our individual differences. We use them to evaluate what to us is personally the right and wrong way to behave. The following personal example from the first author illustrates how values made a difference.

Mike's Story

Growing up, I was unremarkable as an athlete. As an adult, the barrage of media about sports goes right by me. However, in the middle of my life, I sometimes found myself in a leadership role by default, as a soccer coach and then a basketball coach for my then grade-school-age sons. All that I could bring to that role was my organizational skill and a commitment to doing the job well, but almost no athletic knowledge. I geared the activity so that all the boys in the school or community who wanted to play could play. I learned that the kids were capable of remarkable performance when they believed in what they were doing.

Particularly clear in my memory was a basketball game we lost to an especially streetwise, aggressive, and talented inner-city team. The game, scheduled to be played at 8:00 P.M. on a Friday, actually began at 9:00 P.M. Our competitors were very even in their moderate or better skills, where we were very uneven in our abilities, and we appeared tired going into the game that evening. We were an odd mix of very few good players, a handful who were average, and a majority who were not very skilled. This made for a challenge.

As coaches, our preference was to frame the team in such a way as to promote everyone's highest potential on the court. This preference was shared by the majority of the boys, and through their performance, they showed their commitment, even if we lost most of our games. That particular Friday night game was no exception as far as losing was concerned, and yet the quality of the boys' play was remarkable. It was clear that they had hit a momentum where they were all playing to their maximum ability, with five players fully engaged on the court, along with frequent relief from the bench. The point to be made here is that the boys quite obviously believed in the value of their strength as a team, and quite frankly it surprised our challengers, who had snickered during the warm-ups where our lack of depth was obvious. They had to play hard to beat us.

Similarly in life, whether it is a review of the fable of the hare and the tortoise, or the major emphasis of the emotional intelligence literature, that natural strength and aptitude do not necessarily win or lead. Invariably, leaders are people who believe passionately in something. Earlier in work life, it is not always clear what that might be, and yet as a leader you are drawn to a particular line of work, with values that become more apparent with experience.

For myself, I grew up in Eastern Washington, where the major enterprise is agriculture. Many of my relatives were involved in farm-related businesses and all the income I made until age 21 was from working the harvest and preparing crops. Whatever is activating and universal about planting and reaping, working with the seasons and soil appealed to me in a very basic way. I liked the rhythm of it and could observe progress. I worked with people who had like-minded enthusiasm. Many of my current close relationships, including my wife, began in those days. I cared for that work so much that if a farm had been part of my heritage, I am sure I would still be in Walla Walla, Washington.

Given that I knew no farm would be bequeathed to me, I went on to college and earned undergraduate and then later graduate degrees in psychology. Gradually it became clear in my late 20s and early 30s that working with and leading people who work with those struggling in their emotional lives, has great meaning for me. In any obvious way, this is probably an irrational passion. I would at various times stop and ask myself why I was pouring so much energy and personal investment into this work. Can I really explain this passion to myself? Could I ever go home to Eastern Washington and declare to others what drives me in this mental health leadership role? The answer to the former question is "yes," and the answer to the latter question is somewhere between "I don't know" and "probably no."

The "take away" from my story is that with my belief in this work and in my coworkers, I have been able to lead initiatives and endure challenges that otherwise, my Conscientiousness strengths notwithstanding, would not have been possible. My belief in the value of this work has given me a higher ground to work from in dealing with those aspects of my personality and associated leadership style that are underpowered and/or interfering.

Like the pharmacist in the technical/expert leader scenario from the last chapter, we see a person with a passion for her work and a commitment to her followers. In the scenario, she is questioning whether she can keep those values vibrant and activated enough to do her job well in a new environment of mergers and subcontracting. It's difficult to be a robot and function as a leader. To lead and lead well means to operate from a position of great belief and do what otherwise may be difficult to impossible. The value that may be at center stage in your work life may not be a lofty goal. It may be the value of focusing on the quality of people with whom you work as colleagues.

Another example of the impact of values on performance can be seen in the telecommunications industry where parallel, if not competing, work groups have had to pool their strengths and "know how" in order to succeed in an increasingly cross-functional and interorganizational work world. Many of those with the greatest expertise had developed this knowledge within their separate and sometimes isolated community of enterprise. Often this information was very much contextual—not the sort of thing you can go to school to learn or read a book about to gain competency.

Beyond the provincial nature of the knowledge base, local workers are also often characterized by a strong loyalty to their work group. To suddenly shift this expertise from the exclusive domain of one work unit to make it accessible to a larger organization, does not come easily for those oriented to the sense of pride associated with contributing to one's long-standing colleagues. Yet, not surprisingly, those who could lead with this broader understanding are not only increasing the likelihood of success for the new venture, but also substantially enhancing the security and general welfare of their original coworkers. They could no longer look to their separate work efforts as enough to assure success in a work world characterized by mergers, alliances, and other forms of integration.

In summary, we hold the values that are our individualized definition of what is important in our lives, that make it possible for us to function at our peak levels. This in turn means an effective 2nd Language of leadership.

INTERVENTION OPTIONS

At this point, we assume that you have a sense of your 1st Language (natural, intrinsic, tacit knowledge) and 2nd Language (acquired from a baseline of being underpowered) leadership status. With the enabling philosophies, you are working to accept the gifts and limitations in your personality, you recognize your strengths, and you see the value of your values. Now you have information about yourself as a leader and perspective points (enabling philosophy) from which to consider that information. What is the next step?

In moving from information to action, we outline three options: (a) work from your strength for leveraging your weaknesses, (b) design partnerships by complementing yourself with colleagues who have compensating strength, and (c) create alignment between your work and your personality. These are not exhaustive lists of options, and not everyone should get into an action mode. For you, the 2nd Language may be simply information versus an agenda for action. So browse through these possibilities and see what, if anything, fits for you.

Work From Strengths

When we are confronted with gently to fairly harsh brushes with reality where the message is change, it is far more palatable to make the necessary adjustments if we have confidence that we have strengths. That is essentially what we suggest as a first line of response in developing 2nd Language accommodation. This probably is an experience you have had previously. For example, imagine that you are advised that you are not making good use of some aspect of your leadership style, or that a certain style is not working to accomplish the task effectively. You view the communication as either useful information or a loss in how you prefer to see yourself. If you are in a state of awareness about both your strengths and also areas of your behavior where you struggle, then you are less likely to be rocked by what you hear in the way of constructive feedback. Remember, too, leaders hear much more about their styles than the average person hears. We should expect to hear more and it will not all be positive.

On the other hand, despite whatever you may hear critically about your leadership style, if you can always focus on your strength, it takes part of the sting out of the feedback to improve. Once you learn about your areas of limitations and struggle with some of these 2nd Language issues, awareness of the leadership limitations is critical to know how to create followership based on strengths.

Even more specific to this intervention option, individuals are able to use their personality strengths to leverage positive adjustments in those areas of leadership where they struggle or are underpowered.

Up to this point, we have thought of the Big 5 as a discrete and somewhat categorically separate set of personality characteristics. Actually in the real world of direct experience, there is no Big 5. It is simply an abstraction. Furthermore, in the real world, all these personality areas interact with one another. For example, popular leaders who are open to learning from their experiences are more likely to succeed and balance out proclivities toward indirectness and impulsiveness than a person who has weaknesses but no counterbalancing strengths. The same is true for an individual who is an anxious introvert yet dominantly conscientious and passionately committed to his or her profession. This also applies to less than altruistic super stars who are highly aggressive, yet able to shift their strategies to engage workers whose motivations are mostly about survival and social stimulation.

In other words, there is an accumulation of power in leveraging strengths to mitigate weaknesses in people who are motivated to succeed. This type of thinking is actually consistent with what we already know in the personality and management literature. As for personality, one of the perspectives on the Big 5 is to think about the five domains and their facet subparts as a dynamic interactive system. Whereas a number of people have contributed to this so-called "circumplex model," most of the formative work was done by Timothy Leary, who of course is better known for his counterculture activities. In the management field, one-dimensional approaches have been criticized for years, resulting in a pejorative representation of the word *bureaus* as "bureaucratic." We are encouraged in the more flexible, less bureaucratic world of work to be (at the level of workers, managers, and systems) integrated and cross-functional. That model clearly depicts what the 2nd Language represents as a focus. The ideal effective leader does not work from one-dimensional strength but instead applies the full range of potential skill sets to be successful.

LEADERSHIP DEVELOPMENT STRATEGIES

As concrete examples of how to use options, leadership development strategies are presented for the high-achieving leader (who is aggressive and achievement-oriented but relatively inattentive to the needs of others), the expert leader (guided by strict and rigid preferences for how things should be done), and the popular leader (who is agreeable but relatively low in order and self-discipline). Following is an example of how to work from strengths.

Scenario: A High-Achieving Leader

- Recognize and respect your great strength of enthusiasm and energy.
- Transition from the verbs of an "all star" to those of a coach, for example, *orchestrates, motivates, plans collaboratively, manages through others*.
- Begin to direct a portion of time to meeting with staff as individuals and as small groups to clarify their needs and interests.
- Be active in calling out the alignment between their interests and those of the organization. Use this as a frame for assigning and acknowledging their work.
- Register that as with individual performance, even with a skillful mastery, realistic outcomes are a "performance average" and no one is at 100%. Develop a reasonable range of performance for what might be expected from a work team.
- Use a consultant, mentor, or leadership peer group to assist in refining this new skill set.

Design Partnerships

There are times when the demands of the work situation, coupled with the nature and degree of our leadership limitations, call for strategies in addition to working from strengths. Accordingly, it is always desirable to look within your leadership team, or think for that matter about who might be added to it, to complement your strength and weaknesses with their strengths. This may give you balance in your leadership struggles. In our example from chapter 5, the superstar engineer is concerned with the discontinuities between his assertive, goal-oriented style and that of the comparatively less enthusiastic technical staff. His first inclination was to get tough and establish rules, assuming that many staff members weren't trying hard enough. However, by working with some of the key staff members rather than trying to be the one to enforce all of the rules, he learned the value each member of the staff contributed to the whole.

Suggestions from one informal group moved the department to form small teams where members had the freedom to establish policies without strict directives from the leader. Our engineer was impressed with the high performance levels, new ideas, and excitement as the teams functioned smoothly. Because of these colleagues, he is a much better leader than when he was first moved into the leadership position. Partnering with members of the staff in a team structure made a significant difference in the department's progress.

There are additional pluses and minuses to the partnering strategy. The most obvious pluses are that partnering promotes benefits of commitment and team development. Commitment occurs because, assuming you have selected people with aptitude and a value system that become activated by the work, they, like you, are contributing their gifts to an enterprise of worth. You and others recognize them for their accomplishments, and the commitment deepens. The other dimension to this social phenomenon is that these efforts occur in the context of a team, and as proclaimed by Steven Covey, a very constructive interdependence can occur. So the real world proxy for the 2nd Language is a well-functioning team.

The minuses that may evolve with partnering often occur in the area of inadvertently and unconsciously slipping into a bureaucratic division of labor. A complementary balancing of responsibilities is fine, but a bureaucratic division of labor of leadership skills is not. In other words, followers often expect that leaders know enough specifics about all of the work so that they can respond to questions and not always have to defer to others. Followers expect that the leader is direct enough in telling them and others where the business should go and why. They will not accept that the leader would hand off all this work to other team members. This may sound like a very fundamental and unnecessary caveat, yet it is one that is often not followed by leaders at all levels of responsibility. It is very easy to lock in and stay at the level of 1st Language strengths, and to be too busy to do otherwise. This carries the risk of significant leadership perils. Ironically, many leaders find that they experience the greatest level of learning and are the most convincing when they go out to the workers and not only verbally struggle with them about our work life objectives, but also struggle with their 2nd Language leadership challenges of being present and being clear.

As a concrete example of employing the partner-with-others approach, we return to the popularly selected leader scenario. We consider the leadership development strategy she was offered when she saw herself underpowered in conscientious follow-through, where the nature of the job was not going to allow for a gradual acquisition of significant skills that were needed immediately.

Scenario: A Popular Leader

- The empathic and committed style makes you aware both that you are motivated to increase your "follow through" and that this by itself may not be sufficient for success.
- Realize that tendencies toward lack of order and rigor have and will again interfere with performance.

- Consider calling upon your clinic community to participate in a social contract with you, being both frank in advising you when you "fall short" and willing to complement you in structuring the follow through.
- Don't feel compelled to lead. But don't despair either. Like you, two U.S. presidents (Franklin D. Roosevelt and John F. Kennedy) were charismatic populists who initially felt over their heads in their jobs, and yet by dint of compensating personality strengths, challenging experiences, and the support of key allies, matured considerably and performed well. They were far from perfect people, but they were good political leaders.

Create Alignment of Work and Personality

Another name for this strategy of creating alignment is to avoid leadership tasks for which you are not suited. Even in the 2nd Language of Leadership, not all situations will be reasonable for all leaders. Ultimately, there is some unique mix of aptitudes, passions, and personality styles that result in a match or lack thereof for a specific situation. In actuality, to work with this as a basic operating principle can result in less rather than more pain and disappointment for the individual and those who are the followers.

The search for a match may occur during the early stage of adult development. It might occur midstream as noted in the scenario from the last chapter of the well-adjusted technical leader who finds the world has changed around her, requiring that she discern the most appropriate direction for her future. This alignment strategy does not suggest that you are not meant for leadership in general. Instead, alignment strategy represents an approach to consider if you believe in something worthwhile, attempt to make sense of the situation you are in, and are eager to create an environment that motivates others to follow, for then you are a leader. You may not be a formal leader with a designated title, but you are nonetheless leading a meaningful pursuit.

There are a variety of books and experts that will instruct you on how to divide the world into leaders and nonleaders. For example, the book *Certain Trumpets*, by Gary Wills, depicts leaders across a range of fields from art to business to politics. One criticism is that as Wills differentiated the winners and losers in leadership, there was an implicit assumption that the losers were completely without merit.

One of Wills' observations is that Eleanor Roosevelt was categorically different in making the New Deal "real" for those in need in this country in contrast to Nancy Reagan's quasi-scold of "just say no!" (to drugs). However, the question goes back to Mr. Wills' leadership categories and the question of where do these powerful women have a good match between their 1st and 2nd Language strengths and leadership opportunities. It is probably easy to villainize and trivialize Nancy Reagan, but to suggest—albeit implicitly—that she made no leadership contribution is unfair. It also reinforces the main focus on winning and losing versus learning and choosing a match that creates the opportunities for your best contributions.

The idea of contribution and leadership potential is much more the issue here, rather than winning and losing. Winning and losing are absolutely unavoidable in life, and they represent necessary experience for adapting and learning how to select leadership work assignments. However, winning and losing are not pervasive statements about the goodness of specific leaders.

To Gary Wills' credit, many of his mini-biographies highlight how changes in environment and required competencies rendered previously well-matched, dominant strengths strangely out of vogue. In the terminology of this book, there was a shift from well-performing to poorly performing 2nd Language leadership behavior. Certainly, there were 3rd Language derailments as well. Although not in *Certain Trumpets*, Winston Churchill was a brilliant war-time strategist and inspirational leader, yet a peace-time flop as a leader. President Eisenhower had enough range in his style to demonstrate dominate strength in both peace and war leadership. Colin Powell has been represented as having similar potential.

Beyond highlighting the need to determine if the leadership opportunity before you is appropriate and to measure the likelihood that you could offer a contribution, the other point to be made in the alignment strategy is to be attentive to the situational nature of certain leadership circumstances. To that end, the following leadership development strategy from the technical (pharmacy) leader scenario underlines that the leader's previous good match but also encourages gathering enough information in a new and emerging situation to separate out transitional requirements from ultimate requirements. As you may recall, the technical leader's greatest strength is a good adjustment, which has been aided by a willingness to be guided by strict if not rigid preferences about how one thinks about and does one's work.

Scenario: A Technical Leader

- Acknowledge skill and expertise in continuous examination of the psychological compatibility of your life and work choices so that they reinforce competence in taking on predictable complexity versus managing the "slippery slopes" of situational problem solving.
- Given your Adaptiveness, shift the focus from where your understanding is clear knowledge of yourself to where your understanding is not-so-clear turbulence of the environment.
- Let the dust settle in your situation, secure consultation from others who have undergone similar work changes, and clarify what you can about the new expectations as they stabilize. You may find that

the noise of transformational activity may fade into the background, and that the familiar craft of pharmacy may return to the foreground.
- Match up "you" and your preferred "environment," and trust yourself to make the right decision.

SCHEMA AND A FORESHADOWING

Until this point, we have related that there are certain ways of thinking and behaving that increase the likelihood of good leadership outcomes with Big 5 personality data. In the next section, we quickly capsulize those thoughts and actions, and then present them in the overall schema of the 2nd Language of Leadership. The final comments are reserved for foreshadowing the next chapter with its emphasis on discussing what we know about learning effectiveness behaviors.

Once you have Big 5 data, the most useful thoughts are ones of accepting that you have strengths and weaknesses within your personal and leadership style, celebrating your strengths in a practical, nonidealizing way, and discerning the core values you have as a leader. Because of the powerfulness of our core values, they will assist you in the often frustrating experience of managing those parts of your style that are underpowered or interfering with complete effectiveness. Framed as a metaphor, consider leadership development as more like working on a batting average rather than winning the baseball games. These thoughts are meant to address the resilient and hardy part of whom you are. You have to work at leadership. In fact, there will never be a time when you do not have to work at it. Otherwise, leadership would only be a 1st Language exercise.

Leadership effectiveness is learned. No one starts with 1st Language skills straight across the board, and no one can learn leadership to the point that it is an acquired, pervasive 1st Language skill set. Leadership represents a batting average—less than 100%—and the following three thoughts can assist you in setting the stage for effectiveness. To be effective, you need to think and act within the context of the 2nd Language. Consider the following three strategies:

1. Work from your strengths using their potency to increase effectiveness where your personality is underpowered or otherwise interfering. You already do this naturally; do it more.
2. Design partnerships with others whose dominant personality strengths complement you and augment your leadership output through a highly effective team. This counterbalances a tendency to build a team with mirror reflections of you, and this will only work if you continue to work genuinely at your 2nd Language struggles as an individual.
3. Create alignment in your work and personality and use your evolved common sense to look for matches between who you are and what

is required of you in a particular situation. This makes the learning curve less steep in choosing opportunities for making a leadership contribution.

The 2nd Language schema relies on an understanding of a leadership situation from a personality perspective, an accurate reading of your Big 5 status, and the employment of strategies. A personality perspective is understanding the demands on you as a leader, vectored against a historical appreciation concerning what has come easy or difficult for you in using your personality to solve leadership problems. The 2nd Language of Leadership Questionnaire in the Appendix includes a set of questions that may be useful to you in clarifying your leadership effectiveness approaches. A reading of your Big 5 status includes a number of elements that we have reviewed thus far, including a Mini-Marker or NEO–PI representation of traits with variation in their respective strength, a bridge from traits to behavior, and a reformatting of behavior consistent with your unique (five factor profile) contribution to making sense of situations and motivating others to accomplish work.

The three scenarios in chapter 5 parallel these steps in the schema. The remainder of the schema, which takes us full circle, is the content of this chapter: The enabling philosophies, how we think about ourselves, the challenge of leadership, the intervention strategies to determine whether the situation and person are a good match. Should they be a good match, what combination of working from the leverage of one's strengths as well as looking to others to balance weakness will accomplish the goal of leadership?

CLOSING COMMENTS

We are at a stage now where much of the architecture of the *2nd Language of Leadership* is in place. The remaining questions go beyond the issue of possible personality change to address what we know about learning effectiveness behavior and how to set goals to accomplish effectiveness. The next chapter's focus includes the headlines of knowledge accumulated to-date about adults as effective life learners. We also discuss what facilitates the learning process. Although this does not add any particular content to the 2nd Language, it does offer context. The information will give you an idea about how alike or different you are from people who have been able to increase their effectiveness.

Learning to Lead: The Good News

Synopsis

The principal message of *The 2nd Language of Leadership* hinges on the critical premise that effective leadership behavior is a learned competency. The scientific information addressing that specific question is in its early evolution. Nonetheless, good news can be extrapolated from the behavior change literature that provides direction for people who want to learn effective behavior. In addition, a set of conditions exists that make such learning likely to occur.

Effective behavior is learned when it is a focal point and when adults are optimistic and active in acquiring what they perceive as needed development skills. The manner in which competency-based leadership learning takes place fits into the larger arena of the adult-education model. These conditions accelerate learning.

The belief that people learn is an operating assumption underlying all the education and training work that are the product lines of our academic and service-oriented institutions and businesses. Yet, what we know and do not know about how people make adaptive changes in their lives is pretty much a blind spot. To correct for the glibness that often characterizes change or improvement exercises, of which the 2nd Language is one example, this chapter presents: (a) a brief overview of what we know about the effectiveness of behavior change strategies in the counseling literature, (b) a discussion of the conditions that improve the likelihood that desired change occurs, and (c) an attempt to fit this 2nd Language work into a set of activities that is characteristic of the adult-education school of thought.

Why do this? The primary purpose is because enough of you out there may be very skeptical about self-improvement strategies that haven't been framed in some larger, cogent context of science and theory. With the information provided in this chapter, we believe you will have more confidence that the 2nd Language makes sense and fits together in the broader realm of how people learn and change.

SCIENCE OF BEHAVIOR CHANGE

Long before Freud popularized counseling as a method for ameliorating human struggles, people experienced difficulties in their lives and looked to others for help. Therefore, the need for and the history of helpers goes back to the beginnings of recorded life and includes roles of shaman, witch doctors, priests, and so on. With this in mind, it is remarkable that only since the 1980s has there been a systematic, organized review of counseling effectiveness outcome studies. As a point of reference, it is important not to lose sight of the commonality between all effectiveness endeavors, whether it is mental-health counseling or leadership effectiveness training. The common thread is working with people to assist them to function better, perform as improved problem solvers, and so on.

In the early 1980s, Smith and Glass along with their associates published a meta-analysis of many of the counseling studies that had been completed up to that time. A meta-analysis is a research design that measures a consistent way of evaluating the strength of those studies and the rigor of the conclusions. They found, remarkably enough, that virtually all psychotherapeutic and counseling approaches were useful in assisting people to feel more comfortable and function more effectively than they had prior to counseling.

This conclusion appeals to our common sense when we think about what counseling is. Counseling is the work of at least two people interacting in a supportive relationship, where one person is the helper and the other is the helped and the objective is to learn a more adaptive approach. If, for example, depression is the problem state characterized by social withdrawal and negative thoughts, then the intervention is to promote interpersonal activation and constructive interpretation of the individual's experience. In brief, it is intuitively logical that if you work on a problem in a focused way aided by a caring, intelligent human being, the likelihood that the outcomes will be better than not having that level of assistance seems somewhat obvious. However, the implications are substantial. The aim is to develop a focus, find a cogent problem-solving approach, and work with a knowledgeable, caring other. This applies to learning leadership effectiveness training as well.

Those of you who are scientifically minded readers no doubt have additional questions that go beyond the relatively global findings of Smith and Glass. For example, you may wonder if, in the psychiatric literature, there is any differential between general counseling approaches versus specific ones. Certainly that has applicability as a corollary for the 2nd Language strategy. If all intervention, training, and counseling approaches are equivalent, what determines why you would chose one over another? The response to the question is again we are very young in our knowledge about such things. The quality culture encourages us to develop consistent processes that are designed to accomplish specific outcomes and then continually improve the processes based on what we learn from our measurements.

Within psychiatry, we know that certain cognitive behavioral (i.e., focus on learning non- depressive cognitions and behavior) interventions work better than nonspecific "usual care," but even there, we don't know that this approach is the best. Our lack of convictions speaks more to the early stage of this research rather than being a pejorative statement about what we have researched to date. The overall impression is that it is better to have training and counseling interventions geared toward both specific issues and the uniqueness of the person as opposed to being nonspecific, but beyond saying that, we do not know a lot yet about the particulars.

Others of you will also wonder if people might not learn problem-solving approaches on their own without the assistance of counseling. In other words, if I can learn what I need to know without going to counseling, why go? Ken Howard, a psychology professor from Northwestern University, has researched this question in his "dose effect" studies. He and his colleagues found that when you followed up the problem-solving effectiveness of people who had comparable problems, the differences in problem-solving improvement depended on whether or not they participated in counseling. The nature of those differences in the effectiveness of problem solving were very much in favor of those who had participated in counseling: These participants showed 50% effectiveness improvements in 2 months compared to 2% improvement in the same time period for those in comparison groups. Yes, the noncounseling group did show, over a couple of years, similar increments in their problem-solving skill. However, consider how much time had passed!

What those in counseling accomplished in a couple of months, took those who didn't participate in counseling, 2 years to accomplish. The obvious implication is to take advantage of the structure, support, and richness of information that is present in counseling, and you will experience a much less time-consuming and probably less tumultuous trial-and-error experience than you will encounter on your own. We offer you the same inference in relation to learning leadership effectiveness.

Finally, some of you may feel we are pushing the limit to the logical error of limping analogies by using mental-health counseling as a reference for leadership effectiveness improvement. Albeit, what we know is largely anecdotal and not as empirically based as we would like. However, a meta-analysis by Lipsey and Wilson addressed the change process occurring across many behavior change venues including learning performance skills, academic proficiencies, and athletic competencies. The results showed that essentially the same phenomenon occurs across the entire spectrum of behavior change. For example, if you make a particular skill area a focus, introduce a helping expert, and practice a viable approach, you learn much faster than not following this focused work. Although this information is not conclusive, it is substantial enough to satisfy for the moment the requirements set from scientific training. In other words, there are enough analogs out there in the empirical literature to confirm that leadership training makes sense and is worth doing, as opposed to concluding that leadership skills are limited to what people learn exclusively from their experience.

With this behavior change literature as a stage setter, we turn our attention to the conditions that promote change in effectiveness.

Conditions That Promote Change in Effectiveness

Two fundamental questions occur in thoughtful consideration of what is involved in any counseling-oriented behavior change activity. First, what personal characteristics correlate with change? Second, how do people change? Both of these questions (and answers) are important because they are basic to an approach like the 2nd Language. Concretely, what are the things about me, when present, that augur in the direction of achieving desired 2nd Language change? Next, where would I need to be in the change process to experience practical value from this training? Once again, we draw from what we know about these questions from the counseling literature, and then make the principles underlying the learning available for 2nd Language work.

What Correlates With Change?

What personal characteristics correlate with good counseling outcome? As recently as 25 years ago, the so-called YAVIS syndrome was one set of impressions about who does best in counseling. YAVIS essentially stood for those people who are Young–Attractive–Verbal–Intelligent–and–Social. The political correctness, and the validity of such a position, would be very much in question today. Another set of characteristics that describe people in less prejudicial and more respectful terms, that goes beyond incidental and unchangeable variables such as Young and Attractive, includes the concepts of *Expectancy, Necessity* and *Tolerance*.

Those people who appear to profit from a behavior change opportunity are those who have some level of hope and optimism for a positive outcome. This expectancy factor absolutely permeates our experience in life. It goes the range from the teacher (Pygmalion) expectation of student performance studies, to the role of placebo in medicine, to occupied countries freeing themselves from the totalitarian yoke of the Soviet Union, to the demise of apartheid in South Africa. It is the basic antidote to the impression of life as "brutish and short" espoused by the British empirical philosopher, Thomas Hobbes. It balances what we know about the relative presence of negative and positive perceptions about life that differentiates depressed from nondepressed people.

The depressives often offer a starkly realistic assessment of their circumstances. The uniqueness of the nondepressives is their hope and optimism. It is not their youth and attractiveness. Optimism can be learned, and it certainly can be activated in a helping relationship. Without a positive expectation, there are not many miracles in the sphere of effectiveness improvement.

The noted American philosopher and pioneer psychologist/physician, William James, referred to habit as the "great fly wheel of society." We are creatures of habit. Our habits are among the greatest sources of comfort for us in a very dynamic world. The dependability and reliability of our habits do eventually run into the wall of necessity, meaning that our lives are not some continuously static, homogenous thing.

The circumstances of our life change, and then we must change, by necessity. If we do not see the necessity or accept it, we get stuck. Freud called chronic stuckness "fixations." Today, "getting stuck" means temporary interference in some important part of our functioning. When it continues or derails us, it is called a psychiatric disorder. Primarily, getting stuck and not using necessity for its adaptive opportunity means that we are a little less functional than we could be.

The necessity of learning from mistakes and considering them an opportunity are key factors in behavioral change. In addition, there is a necessity of adapting to a changing environment and seeing it as a chance for survival and success if we are to experience change. Most of us are not always in a posture of smiling anticipation either about what will go wrong next that can be seen as a gift or what will be required of us that will be our next challenge (euphemism for problem). In reality, we will need to have a certain amount of *tolerance* to work ourselves through the necessary adjustment and accommodation to a new situation.

The frustration–aggression hypothesis is a well-known principle in psychology, where with increasing, unmitigated frustration, we can expect increased distress, irritation, and potentially aggression. This is also consistent with the Adaptiveness domain of the Big 5, specifically the Angry–Hostile facet, which we have constructively renamed Serenity, and which more accurately looks more like Frustration/Irritability when you read the NEO–PI test questions.

What mitigates against frustration is tolerance, and what helps with tolerance is a positive expectancy and a sense of necessity. The combination of these acquirable behaviors and perspectives is the equivalent of hardiness and resilience. Tolerance does not stand on its own. We can build it if we see a necessity and a basis for hope.

This combination of personal features that correlate with good psychotherapy outcome are transcendent in their applicability to constructive change in life. They are mostly congruent with our implicit psychology of how people in the natural course of their lives adapt, adjust, and cope, and when circumstances are most optimal, where they may perform at a level where they feel most alive and complete as human beings.

Specific to us and the 2nd Language approach, these three characteristics represent a set of features to be aware of as we strive to accomplish what is important to us. How easily you can call up these features on any given day varies. They are more coordinates on an emotional map than points of performance that we must achieve. Expectancy, necessity, and tolerance serve as guides from which we can chart our course and clarify what is possible and reasonable. In other words, a low necessity reading is a "no starter." High necessity can be a stimulus for activating what we can call up in the way of optimism (expectancy) and its close relative, tolerance. Without this type of assessment, it is difficult to become motivated to do 2nd Language work.

How Do People Change?

If the conditions that correlate with change make up the horizontal axis on the chart of effectiveness efforts, then the sequential process of how people change is on the vertical axis. Why is it important for you to know how people change? This knowledge clarifies what stage of change you may be in, so that you can consider what your needs are and what they are not. In the next section, we flesh out the concept of how people change and then its applicability here will become more apparent.

Studies of how people change have been useful in shedding light on how we go through a process of becoming aware of a change possibility before we begin to conceptualize it, let alone begin to gather information about it. Subsequently, we may try out new behaviors, evaluate our experience, make modifications, gather new information, and so on. In actuality, the change process is probably not that linear. However, it is compelling to consider that most effective learners will evaluate an idea for its cogency and relevance to him or her before they move in the direction of devoting time and energy into learning more about a problem-solving strategy. Similar to a counseling scenario, where we are working with someone who is essentially browsing and not buying, the same is true with the 2nd Language. It would be wise to make information available as it is requested and not advance the discussion prematurely to action planning.

The experience from conducting workshops on the 2nd Language is that people tend to be 50–50 as to whether they fall into the category where information as opposed to action is their focus. Workshops are probably not the same magnet for necessity as mental-health counseling or requested individual consulting for leadership effectiveness would be. The backdrop assumptions about the readers of this book are that you might be in: (a) a preconceptualization mode (haven't thought about the personality aspects of leadership effectiveness before; I will read and see what the idea is); (b) the information mode (OK, I get the idea; I would like to know more about how this might relate to me); (c) the action mode (I want to apply this to a specific situation I am dealing with); or (d) either a reflection or maintenance/improvement phase (I am using 2nd Language strategies, and I am evaluating how they worked for me and how to make them work better).

In summary, where our personal variations of optimism, sense of necessity, and personal tolerance determine the likelihood that we will make desired changes, there is another dimension of how people change that is sequential in nature. Awareness of where we are in the change process (relative to needs for information, direction, etc.) can make it easier to chart and set realistic expectations for how we get from here to there. Both of these considerations are very important in increasing 2nd Language effectiveness.

ADULT-EDUCATION APPLICATIONS

This last section of the chapter is an attempt to pull out all that has been communicated to you about the science, conditions, and process of behavior change; and then to use this information and place it within the context of education, and specifically, adult education.

All of us have taken the classes that were required for graduating with whatever degrees we have pursued. For many of us, these classes were requirements in a very external way. They were other peoples' requirements of us. These were not courses that included content that was either of interest to us; nor by completing them were we prepared in any particular way to perform better in a trade or craft. Such are the memories of much of high school and college.

The field of adult education is categorically different. Adult education is sought out because it means something very specific and internal to an individual. This is the way we think of people learning the 2nd Language approach. It is about their jobs and their leadership role within that job. Learning leadership behavior is inclusive of many of the elements that are true in learning improved life-adaptive skills in counseling. Yet, the 2nd Language training endeavors exist more on the plane of adult education. Your understanding of the elements of adult education is another perspective point from which you can consider the employment of the 2nd Language approach.

Threefold Approach of Adult Education

First, unlike many areas of traditional academic education, the participant in adult education has experience in the area of study. This is true for the person learning the 2nd Language perspective because the training usually draws people who are in leadership roles or have been in them and are considering re-engaging leadership responsibilities. Unique to leadership training and contrasted with continuing professional education for professions-based licensure or recertification, many people have never had academic training in leadership.

Second, not only have the participants had experience in the area of study, but they typically enter the class with specific questions. Consistent with our intent in the 2nd Language workshop, participants are at least in the cognition phase of change and want specific information.

Third, in adult education, because the course work is of practical importance, the participants often have a desire to move from information to action. This dovetails with a basic principle of behavior change, which is to evaluate what you are doing now. Even contrasting your current process in comparison to another (i.e., 2nd Language) begins to set into motion a change (however minimal) in how you operate. On the other end of the continuum, some individuals attending 2nd Language workshops utilized the time in class as literally an intense preparation and rehearsal exercise to deal with a specific situation that needed to be addressed immediately.

Succinctly, the 2nd Language approach in a workshop format is of course more like adult education than any other way of looking at it. Ongoing, life-long education in professional responsibilities is typical for adults, and the 2nd Language content is a reasonable adjunctive way of becoming better prepared for mastering the leadership dimension of your chosen craft.

CLOSING COMMENTS

The good news about learning to lead is that people change in ways that are consistent with their desires and preferences. Although the whole science of behavior change is in its infancy, it is reasonable to extrapolate that leadership effectiveness includes the same principles of change that we see operating with other venues for increasing personal effectiveness. In fact, the personal features that optimize counseling outcomes are probably present in spades for leaders. They have a positive expectancy that change is very possible; there are a set of circumstances that makes change if not necessary then certainly desirable; there is a realism that while going from the familiar to the unfamiliar in learning new effectiveness behaviors, a level of tolerance helps. In respectful consideration to where people are in the process of change, we know that you need to conceive an idea before you are ready to assimilate information, let alone begin action planning.

Finally, although reading a book is mostly a conceptual exercise, people who participate in 2nd Language training are in the most fundamental way participating in adult education. They know the area (leadership), they have questions, and they often have a need to transfer information into action quickly.

As we are covering the last laps here, the following chapters include a review of how you can translate this information into goal setting and how you might think about leadership effectiveness, if the problem solving is temporarily, yet nonetheless substantially derailed (3rd Language). Finally, we discuss what might be the next step for those who want something beyond this book as a 2nd Language experience.

2nd Language Goal Setting

Synopsis

Goal setting is a process of converting information into intentions and then developing a system to achieve them. This chapter clarifies the value of goal setting, identifies the characteristics that are associated with successful goal setting, and includes both a Goal Process Matrix (GPM) and a Goal Outcome Matrix (GOM) that operationalize the specific steps taken to be successful. An example is offered about how this might apply to a 2nd Language strategy. This set of information is one way of making the shift from awareness to action in employing your 2nd Language strategy.

The model of goal setting in the chapter offers a specific methodology that you might draw from and that has proven to be useful in a number of scientific studies about what works in goal setting. We build a bridge between the "good news" of the previous chapter that leadership effectiveness can be learned.

TO SET OR NOT SET GOALS?

Goal setting is the hand off from the level of cognitive awareness (I see this is a personality-based opportunity for increasing leadership effectiveness) to the realities of action planning (This is how I will proceed with this opportunity), and it is consistent with the discussion of how people change. Please keep in mind that not all individuals have the same problem-solving styles. What we offer in the book may not fit some styles as comfortably as it does others. We say this because after many years of working with individuals, it is impressive to see the ways people move into action.

Some people are very intuitive and move into action more on a feeling. They operate seemingly without a mapped-out approach, yet in their own way they are taking a step at a time. When asked, these people report a sense that they are proceeding with a broad gestalt. That is, they are adding specifics on an incremental basis to their basic understandings. In contrast, there are those who want the structure and specificity of a goal-setting process. The structure makes the work more real and more approachable. From the structure view, the intuitive types are jumping out of airplanes without checking that the parachute will work. The intuitives see the goal setting of the structured types as a straitjacket of conformity and constrained creativity.

In keeping with the introductory comments at the beginning of the book, this chapter, like the others, can be used as a stand alone section. The intuitive types among you may choose to overlook the specifics and detailed steps that we prescribe. The structured types will follow these steps, with lots of underlining and notes in the margin of the two matrix processes. For those who are in between, a skimming of the content may be useful as a reference in forming your action plans. In other words, there may be bits and pieces that appeal to you.

The remainder of the chapter is divided into four sections. First, we discuss the purpose of goal setting, followed by the characteristics of successful goals. Next, we examine the two goal matrices, one for setting up the process we refer to as GPM and the other for tracking the outcomes we refer to as GOM. Finally, we provide an example to demonstrate how to use the goal-setting tools.

PURPOSE OF GOAL SETTING

Generally, goal setting is important because it introduces order into an activity that is otherwise relatively amorphous, either because we have not done it before or because we have not done it systematically. Accordingly, setting goals directs behavior, leads to higher performance levels, and affords us something to measure against progress. In directing and measuring goals, we are clarifying what is important to us. Within the 2nd Language approach, we are identifying where, developmentally, we want to increase our competence and mastery. Therefore, the broadest description of goal setting is that it is both the blueprint and the scaffolding for personal development and, in this case, leadership development.

Despite our style of problem solving and regardless of how structured or intuitive we may be, goal setting (within the broad confines of what has been described) is what we do if we want to make changes that have a reasonable chance of occurring and being sustained. That is, however, if certain conditions exist.

CHARACTERISTICS OF SUCCESSFUL GOALS

Life experience gives us a sense of which plans people set into motion have a chance of succeeding and which ones will never get off the ground. You will find the following characteristics of successful goals to be in keeping with your implicit standards of what you would need to see in an action plan that would pass the threshold of viability for success. To be successful, goals need to have five characteristics. These include being (a) specific, (b) measurable, (c) achievable, (d) realistic, and (e) time related. A simple way to remember the characteristics of goals is to think about setting SMART goals (e.g., *Specific*, *Measurable*, *Achievable*, *Realistic*, and *Time* related). Let's look more specifically at each goal characteristic.

Specific

Specific goals are clear and accurately defined. For example, you can express an interest or need explicitly, such as participating in a team meeting by voicing your opinion. Or you can be specific concerning which aspects of your Big 5 personality profile will come into play and exactly what it is that you hope to do by employing 2nd Language strategy. Specific means basically precise and tangible.

Measurable

In a complementary fashion, establishing a specific goal also means that you have to be able to document and measure to what extent the goal, or progress toward the goal, has been made. What, precisely, are you hoping to achieve? Without a type of yardstick or measurement indices, your progress (or lack of progress) cannot be tracked. Determining the tool for measurement is often one of the most difficult aspects of goal setting because leadership behaviors are rarely completely objective.

Realistic

Realistic goals are ones that have a manageable balance between what you think you can do and what is possible. Units of work need to be identifiable. For example, a task can be broken into steps that are manageable. Goals established using these criteria are guided by what you are interested in, content wise, and equal to in the way of aptitude (Big 5 and related intellectual strengths). As you will read in the example, goal setting needs then to be realistic to who you are. In Big 5 terms, it means you are not going to completely change your personality. However, you can focus on specific aspects and learn to work with your strengths and limitations.

2ND LANGUAGE GOAL SETTING

Another perspective of establishing realistic goals is that you need to consider the degree to which a situation or person is under your control. In terms of internal and external dimensions, what can you orchestrate as it applies to a particular situation? Most simply, this involves being able to put onto your visual screen what is possible, recognizing that there are limits to what you are able to control in the way of external events or other peoples' behavior. Yet, you are able to influence both events and people.

It is realistic to consider goals related to events that you can influence and most specifically how the events may unfold and how people may think and behave. Bringing this control matter into a 20/20 acuity of focus is crucial to accomplishing a goal. For example, you may own several computer retail stores that have had increasing success for the past 8 years. As the economic trends have been pointing to less retail sales and greater E-commerce, you realize you cannot change the economic environment and reality of the Internet. However, in a clear and realistic way you have the opportunity to adapt pieces of new technologies so that they are compatible with local customer needs while keeping within the realities of financial independence. Additionally, you can set goals for assisting the customers to move into some more systematic processes of reaching out and further exploring new computer technology. Depending on how skillful your deployment and execution are in that goal setting, it is realistic to consider that you will have influence (control) over a segment of the market, but certainly not all of it.

Control is another one of those constructs like batting averages. No one bats 1.000, but .300s are possibly under your control if you are realistic about your aptitudes, clear about your strategy and destination, and take on a goal that is achievable.

Achievable

Achievable goals are those that are considered to be moderately challenging. These goals are the attainable middle ground between pursuing a level of performance that is beyond your reach, on the one hand, and taking on a project that is so easy and relatively unimportant that it perpetually drops from your list on the other hand. Achievable, moderately challenging goals invigorate us because they are doable. They advance our developmental agenda. Their progress makes a difference in some incremental fashion in being a more masterful leader by drawing from your strengths and limitations to accomplish valued outcomes. Leadership goals that leverage our personality strengths and/or complement the strengths of others are achievable; goals that unduly draw on areas of strength where we are weak, may very well not be achievable.

Time Related

The last of the five characteristics of successful goals is the relationship with time. Although establishing specific, measurable, achievable, and realistic goals is important, you also need to develop a time line. It is not enough to just set a goal without recognizing that a checkpoint needs to be planned as to when the goals will be achieved. Or, you can create several checkpoints along the way to stop and assess your progress. Will it be 2 weeks, 3 months, within a year?

It is obvious that the characteristics of successful goals overlap and are subject to a variety of different interpretations. However, in aggregate they serve as a litmus test of sorts that tells us whether it is worth preceding or not, with a goal of increasing personality-oriented leadership effectiveness.

GOAL MATRICES

In the next section, we explain the GPM and the GOM and will concurrently walk you through an example of how to apply these tools to a specific situation. We present an example of the first author's own goal-setting regime.

The GPM is one way of thinking through how you might decide what your goal is and how you will proceed to accomplish it. The steps of the GPM are illustrated in Fig. 8.1. The GOM is a way to check your progress and determine your reinforcement system. We'll first examine the GPM.

GPM

The GPM is a working document that helps you establish a written strategy for each specific behavior that you are committed to modifying or enhancing. Once you have developed the matrix, you will have begun working on your progress toward accomplishment. You will see this specifically as we parallel the description of each of the seven steps with content in Mike's action plan to increase the frequency and effectiveness of participation in team meetings.

The seven steps are as follows:

Step 1: Goal and Purpose. First, create a goal that meets the criteria we discussed earlier. That is, the goal is specific, achievable, and realistic. Indicate whether the goal is directed toward a new area of interest or responsibility that you want to develop or whether it is an area of established strength that you want to further reinforce or enhance. Also, articulate the purpose of the goal relative to your 2nd Language desire to make improvements within the Big 5 conceptualization of leadership.

Mike's Example. My goal is to hold two clinic meetings per month during which I will update staff about department developments and hear their concerns and recommendations. The purpose of this goal is to

Goal and Purpose *(Create SMART goals; articulate purpose relative to 2nd Language)*		
Priority *(Explain or rank importance)*		
Leverage Strategies *(Identify, be explicit; partner to increase impact)*		
Schedule of Activities *(Outline steps, identify assistance)*		
Measurement *(Establish objective, quantifiable standards, measures)*		
Time Frame *(Establish realistic time line for accomplishment)*		
Sustainability *(Implement mechanisms to maintain progress, success)*		

FIG. 8.1. Goal Process Matrix (GPM).

strengthen the team's commitment to our work by increasing clarity of communication and understanding and by being physically responsive.

In Big 5 terms, the 2nd Language strategy is to be more straightforward and clear (less indirect and ambiguous), and more gregarious (less isolated). This activity of participating in staff meetings is one I want to improve upon through the frequency and quality of my presence, and I look to my strengths with conscientious dedication to assist me.

Step 2: Priority. Without priorities, goals have no particular status. The relative importance of a goal directs its actions and the efforts proportionately.

Mike's Example. Both attending these meetings and achieving the 2nd Language improvement in my personal leadership style is a high priority. I see the importance in the health care industry of including my coworkers in the clinical teams with more information and personal contact from me. The teams are experiencing a time of unprecedented upheaval with downsizing and shifting markets and products. This is a time where regular and personal communication with staff is a high priority. The security of information and good relationships with leaders must counterbalance the lack of security in continuous employment. In addition, good communication increases the likelihood staff will see a cogent business approach and engage it.

> Step 3: Leverage Strategies. It is necessary to be explicit and clear about leverage strategies. Identify them so that you are conscious of how you are employing areas of much appreciated strength, stretching capacity in underdeveloped and/or weak areas, partnering with other to increase net impact, keeping centered and emotionally fueled by your values.

Mike's Example. Although team meetings can be uncomfortable for me (emotional reactiveness, anxious, irritable) given their occasional unpredictable course, I recognize this type of dialogue is absolutely essential to success. Accordingly, as in other times in my life where difficult challenges loomed before me, my ability to draw from a conscientious behavior pattern has seen me through to survival, if not success. It is important to anchor my presence with my strong belief in the team-based delivery work we do, and the value of and significance of working with professional staff who assist people who struggle with emotional issues in their lives. This has sustained me before and will sustain me again. Accompaniments from other department leaders who complement my strengths and weaknesses helps as well.

Think back to our story of The Popcorn Chronicles in chapter 1 and Joe's experience of sitting through the meetings with Dianne and her employees. At first Joe considered the meetings to be a waste of time. He was unable to make a formal presentation and direct the action of the meetings with his voice useless because of the popcorn he had consumed. Later, he learns that being present and listening, although not his leadership style, was an aspect of his personality that was affecting his leadership effectiveness.

> Step 4: Schedule of Activities. This step makes it clear how you will plan to improve your performance. It outlines what orchestrating must be done to be successful, including identifying

sources for assistance, and how you will use support to guide and encourage your efforts.

Mike's Example. My experience with teamwork has shown how practice, coordination, and consultation are important elements of scheduling. Practice means to prepare comments in advance and to rehearse before the meeting. Coordination includes working with my secretary and the team leader to get the meeting on the books, and to send out a note to the staff to remind them of the meeting and its purpose. Some staff members become apprehensive about the objective of the meeting. In the absence of clarity, people have assumed that I may be coming to bring bad news. Consultation can include a number of activities. I may give a "dry run" to the administrative staff and ask for feedback. I can call before the meeting and ask key leaders (both formal and informal) from the team about what is on the minds of others. If I am aware that either what I am bringing them or what they may say to me will be a "hot topic," I may seek consultation to assure that my emotionality and indirectness do not interfere with useful communication.

> Step 5: Measurement. Establish how to measure the objective and subjective aspects of accomplishing the goal. For example, will you ask for feedback from peers, subordinates, clients, and partners? Is there is an objective, quantifiable aspect to the goal such as any form of frequency or intensity standard to against which measure?

Mike's Example. On the objective side, the goal is to hold rotating team meetings, among the 12 teams, scheduled so there are two meetings per month. As for subjective input, I will ask the staff to complete a form addressing the usefulness of the meeting. This will include questions such as "on a scale of 1 to 10 rate the meeting and its usefulness; suggest how the meetings be improved." Informally, I can ask selected trusted and frank colleagues to provide me with their perceptions and recommendations concerning my emotionality, directness, clarity, and sociability.

> Step 6: Time Frame. Establish a time frame that realistically projects when the goal can be accomplished, or as more often it is the case in personal development, when you expect desired progress will have been made.

Mike's Example. Within 6 months, I expect to hold 8 meetings. Although 12 meetings would be optimal, it is not realistic in a world where the unanticipated exigencies in the team's schedule and my schedule change our plans. Over the course of those meetings and especially the last 4, I would expect to find a notable improvement in the staff's feedback concerning usefulness. I would also expect that the informal feedback I have asked for from my colleagues would have noted that I used some of their recommendations and that they observed improvements in my emotionality, clarity, and sociability.

Step 7: Sustainability. With the assumption that your goal may be an activity to incorporate into your ongoing practice of leadership, you will want to implement mechanisms for sustaining and maintaining your process and gains.

Mike's Example. In my experience, the following types of mechanisms have been helpful: (a) Formalize the process for scheduling and organizing the meetings; (b) create a log (to be added to over time) of my own and staff observations about what makes team meetings useful; (c) document in a diary the feedback people have given to me that has been helpful in improving my performance; (d) before each meeting, work with my secretary to assure that the scheduling process has been maintained; and (e) review the log and diary before each meeting.

Goal Outcome Matrix

The GOM is the second working document on which to record progress and accomplishments. It is important to document success as you continue to work toward greater leadership effectiveness. Finally, don't neglect to consider the value of rewards. Rewards can be powerful motivators that provide positive feedback and enhance self-esteem. The GOM is illustrated in Fig. 8.2.

The four steps of the GOM are listed below and are framed within the specific example we have been reviewing:

Step 1: Identify Goal. My goal is to schedule two team meetings per month with the expectation that within 6 months I will have participated in eight meetings. I am also committed to increase my awareness and mastery of leadership effectiveness as it relates to my emotionality, gregariousness, and clarity.

Step 2: Report Progress. I will keep a frequency count of attended meetings, track the trends of how useful the staff finds the meetings, and attend to the comments my colleagues offer me concerning my personal progress as a leader with 2nd Language challenges.

Identify Goal		
Report Progress *(Track specific activities that have been undertaken)*		
Document Accomplishments *(Compare progress; assess improvements in 2nd Language strategies)*		
Reward and Reinforce *(Encourage yourself with positive rewards; look for external feedback & reinforcement)*		

FIG. 8.2. Goal Outcome Matrix (GOM).

Step 3: Document Accomplishments. I will compare the progress report against the specific goals of eight meetings in 6 months, and assess incremental improvement in the meetings utility to staff over time, in the hope that my 2nd Language strategy has been specifically (emotionality, sociability, and clarity) successful, and that the process and improvements are becoming routinized and sustained.

Step 4: Reward and Reinforce. I can control an internal reward such as going to lunch at a favorite restaurant after the team meetings or planning on a mushroom hunt or a fishing trip that I will associate with completing this goal successfully. Externally, I can consider that this goal of meeting with teams converges with a core part of my job, and that I will hear how I have been perceived (team communication-wise) in my annual performance evaluation. In the hope that the feedback will be positive, that certainly is an important reinforcement.

The most crucial piece of knowledge and one that has greater poignance and personal value would come if my colleagues determine that I have assisted them in doing their job better. Many of them know what comes easy and hard for me. To the extent that they see my 2nd Language effort as something worthwhile in conducting their mental-health work, that is a very powerful experience for me.

CLOSING COMMENTS

The chapter has introduced you to the useful tool of goal setting so that you can begin to consider the 2nd Language strategy in the context of how people successfully set and accomplish goals. For some, the content will serve as a template you quickly review as you transition your increasing awareness of how to get the best yield from your self as a leader into action. For others, to get started and perhaps to keep going, we suggest you begin using the GPM and GOM.

Within the scope of what we have set out to accomplish by way of communicating an idea, the book is finished. The remaining chapters treat related ideas and actions. Chapter 9 focuses on the 3rd Language of Leadership, where, in a concerning way, a portion of the leader's behavior is dysfunctional. Our objective in that chapter is to make it clear that this is not a rare phenomenon, but rather a common one that can respond to a 2nd Language remedy. The final summary chapter is an introduction to how we could work directly together through workshops and/or an individual consultation. Although obviously this has a marketing quality to it, the intent is to begin to map out a logical progression of work beyond this book.

3rd Language

Synopsis

Whereas 2nd Language struggles are universal in life and leadership, 3rd Language events, centered around mild to moderate psychiatric conditions, are commonplace. In this chapter, we attempt to demystify such problems and their predisposing personality traits as they interface with people in leadership roles. Interventions that would be helpful in such situations are offered that include 2nd Language strategies. The two examples are a leader with an adjustment disorder and a leader with a major depressive disorder. Concluding comments are made concerning the interlinking of 1st, 2nd, and 3rd Languages of leadership.

WHY DISCUSS THE 3RD LANGUAGE?

Although choosing to focus this book on the universality of the 2nd Language perspective, it is artificial to suggest that the world is made up of people who struggle to balance and optimize their strengths and weaknesses, but never really stumble, fall down, and get hurt in the process. The fact is that this does happen often. Although 3rd Language struggles of working with leaders dealing with psychiatric disorders merits a book of its own, we are settling for a chapter. The intent is to provide you—should this issue be your specific concern—with a place to directly go in this book.

We are also framing the 3rd Language situation from the 2nd Language perspective. This means several things. Like the 2nd Language construct, the 3rd Language leadership scenario is a variation of the sequential impact of a situation, personality characteristics, and leadership behavior. In this case, the behavior is not very effective, and it is dysfunctional.

Dysfunctional means there are a number of behaviors that are not working well to solve leadership challenges. The behaviors present may be evident for being withdrawn, abrasively aggressive, anxious, confused in thinking, depressed, and so on. On the remedy side of the equation, 2nd Language strategies are part of the solution to a 3rd Language problem, and a 3rd Language problem may often be an entrée to 2nd Language learning and adjustment. This is especially true when the 3rd Language pain and disability are reduced.

In the following pages, we make the case for the commonality of 3rd Language occurrences (psychiatric disorders encountered by leaders), discuss remedies that include 2nd Language strategies as one element, and review several examples. Next, we summarize with a perspective point that maintains the differences among 1st, 2nd, and 3rd Language forms of leadership while highlighting the real world systematic interrelationships of all three.

Psychiatric Conditions in Leadership

Although the principal reference point for considering the incidence and prevalence of psychiatric disorders are population studies, there is no reason to be assured that people in leadership positions have some special psychological immunity. In fact, the opposite may be the case.

Most of what we know about population occurrence of psychiatric disorders has been studied by National Institute of Mental Health (NIMH) through the Epidemiological Catchment Area (ECA) study initiated during the Carter administration and the Medical Outcome Studies conducted by Rand in the 1970s and 1980s. Although there are many ways to summarize and represent the data, the headlines state that within any year approximately 20% of Americans experience a psychiatric disorder and that the lifetime prevalence is approximately two times this, or approximately 40%. This means that more than 50 million Americans in a given year and upward of 100 million over the course of a lifetime experience the discomfort and disorientation of these conditions. In contrast to the assumptions those of us had growing up in the 1950s and 1960s, psychiatric problems are very common disorders. We are vulnerable to these disorders because of both biologically predisposed personality patterns and developmental complications with life experiences.

Of all these disorders, anxiety and depression are most common. Their symptomatic expressions cluster around behaviors like distress, difficulty concentrating, problems sleeping, lethargy, worry, confused thinking, agitation, and so on. The principal differentiation for anxiety is that it is phenomenologically structured around a fearful anticipation of loss, whereas the psychological experience of depression is that losses have occurred and they feel painfully unresolvable. The majority of adult psychiatric conditions, evidenced both as symptoms and disorders, are a variation of anxiety and depressive states.

Another snapshot of the common nature of these conditions can be seen through the lens of the Center for Health Studies (at Group Health Cooperative of Puget Sound) research, which shows that 20% of adult patients who seek care from their personal physician have a diagnosable behavioral disorder related to depression. About 70% of us go see the family doctor annually. Often our presenting concern is related to depression, or physical symptoms that depression may accompany. In any given year, out of 100 patients who enroll in the health plan, 12 will come in for depression care, half of them with major depression and half with minor depression. For those with major depression, between 50% and 75% of these patients have had prior episodes. So, enough said, there are a lot of these 3rd Language issues occurring out there in the world.

3rd Language Vulnerabilities of Leaders

Again there is no reason to think that simply because you are in a position of leadership you have protection from these psychiatric conditions. Based on the discussion in previous chapters, about both the unique demands of leadership (ranging from managing the daily complexity of work life to being the point person for change), and the unfortunately high failure rate with people in leadership roles, you could say that the role promotes anxiety and often results in depression. This is especially true during the earlier stages in a leader's life and hence that is one of the reasons why we are writing this chapter.

To discuss the occurrence of 3rd Language leadership dysfunctions, it is important to clarify the conceptual foundations of the approach. This is not a chapter about making judgmental determinations of who is and is not suitable for leadership based on personality and adjustment factors. The perspective of the book comes much more from a growth and development model than organizing around a personnel selection process.

Ted Millon, a leading personality theorist, has described (invoking a medical model metaphor) personality to be functionally like our immune system. Some people have strong immune systems. They are quite hardy and resilient. Most people have adequate systems, and a few have ones that are selectively or pervasively weak. So it goes with personality. Building on Millon's thinking and focusing on the vulnerability and strengthening of personality, it is our observation that you are able to increase the hardiness of your personality in proportion to its beginning strength. This is psychologically a form of "the rich get richer." Those who begin with strong systems have more potential to strengthen their personality further than those whose personality system was not strong initially. You might think of the 2nd Language strategy as a personality effectiveness callisthenic behavior. 3rd Language states occur where the immune system of the personality–leadership effectiveness connection is underperforming, stalled, or impaired.

Daniel Levinson's work on adult development offers another window from which to consider this issue of personality development and leadership effectiveness and dysfunction. Levinson and his colleagues wrote the scholarly and popularly acclaimed *Seasons* series including *The Seasons of a Man's Life* and *The Seasons of a Woman's Life*. The books chronicle the respective development, moratoriums, and decline of several groups of people (including a leadership group) dependent on their use of a life structure (equivalent to personality and value systems) and the successfulness (or lack thereof) of their experience across time and in response to sequential developmental challenges. 2nd Language interventions are strategies for bolstering life structures, another construct for personality development. The 3rd Language concept is like an urgency code that signals that the individual leader is in a state of disequilibrium such that leadership effectiveness behavior can be described at best as being in moratorium, at worst in decline.

3rd Language scenarios are crises. Although they destabilize us and are potentially dangerous (to invoke the Chinese symbol and to consider the leader failure rate), they are also an opportunity for significant learning about yourself, your leadership potential (in a dramatic sense what you are or are not good at, what you should learn, and what you should avoid), and life. The danger in 3rd Language situations includes the potential for not only greater and prolonged psychiatric difficulty, but also a premature closing off of leadership. The irony is that the 3rd Language situation is among the clearest and most poignant calls to adjustment in general, as well to a specific form of adjustment—leadership effectiveness employing the 2nd Language strategy. In other words, what upset the apple cart in the situation where a leader began to demonstrate the psychiatric symptoms of 3rd Language dysfunctional leadership behavior (became withdrawn, avoidant, over-reactive) typically represents an imbalance between the demands of a situation and what one brings in the way of personality strengths. Beyond professional help to assist in the acute state of 3rd Language dysfunction, the longer term remedies are to strengthen your personality expression, which is essentially the 2nd Language strategy.

3rd Language Examples

Two fictional yet typical scenarios offer some concrete, real-life examples of 3rd Language leadership situations, without launching into a treatise about psychotherapy for psychiatric conditions. Scenario 1 is a general variety adjustment disorder with mixed disturbance in mood. We describe a person who has functioned well in the past but for several months has experienced a specific stressor that has upset her leadership functioning, as evidenced with mild signs of anxiety and depression. Scenario 2 relates to the less common but far from infrequent major depressive disorder. In Scenario 2 the mood discomfort is more severe, the time of onset is recent, and the functioning is much more impaired. The good news is that major depression is eminently treatable. We have organized the scenarios as follows: the job, the leadership situation, the stressor/personality, the psychiatric condition, the psychotherapy, and the 2nd Language strengthening strategy.

Scenario 1

Rhonda is a 28-year-old female computer-store manager. This is the first store she has managed, having previously held a line job in one of the chain's larger downtown stores. She was chosen for this job when the previous manager suddenly left his position for a better opportunity. Rhonda was asked to fill in with the expectation that she would continue in the role because she was such a good salesperson who was held in high esteem as an informal leader among her coworkers. The most difficult aspect of the new job was that she needed to set the work schedule and assure that the store was covered from 9:00 A.M. to 10:00 P.M. Monday through Saturday. In an effort to form a good relationship with her new employees, she agreed to work shifts for them if the work schedule was a complication in their personal lives. Unfortunately, this effort to win favor with the staff occurred at the expense of the store's not being adequately covered. After several months, the volume of sales dipped and there was a series of service complaints. The primary issue was that she did not have evenings covered well enough and that was when the greatest number of customers was present.

As the manager, Rhonda was held responsible and criticized by her supervisors for this performance problem. Her new work associates did not speak up for her. Not surprisingly, she became exhausted and demoralized by all the long hours and the unsuccessful experience. Although far from being devastated, her energy was down and she was not sleeping well. She was painfully aware of the outcome problems with revenue and service, yet she did not know what to do to resolve her difficulties. The state of being run down did not lend itself to her feeling especially creative in problem solving. These features are consonant with the commonplace adjustment disorder.

Rhonda had experienced these stressors within the developmental and personality circumstances of never having been in a role of formal accountability before where she needed to be firm as well as supportive with coworkers. Her difficulties fall into a familiar rookie pattern where she has overperformed as an individual, her colleagues were not given adequate expectations, and her supervisors underprepared her.

Rhonda's history indicated that she had been characteristically conscientious with many extroverted features that included assertiveness. However, when uncertain of what was expected of her, her first line of response had always been to work hard, and only firmly implement expectations with others when she became more clear in her understanding of a given situation. As for psychotherapy, should Rhonda have pursued it, she would have been advised to reconceptualize her experience for its useful orienting value, especially around the connections and boundaries with coworkers when one is the boss. She would have been encouraged to work out an improvement plan that she could initiate with her supervisors to turn the performance and outcomes around. She could suggest a time period that was reasonable to the supervisors and realistic for her to regain her energy. As a footnote, many people do not go to formal psychotherapy for this type of problem, preferring to receive informal guidance from a friend or a respected person knowledgeable about the work world.

The 2nd Language strategy here, designed both for preventing this from happening again and for strengthening the personality style of an already characteristically strong person, would include the theme of balancing strengths and weaknesses and broadening openness for useful information. In Rhonda's situation, a suggestion would be that although Conscientiousness is her strength, awareness that she is overusing it, as noted recently, probably signals that she needs to be more assertive (Extraversion behavior) in the "self versus other" dimension of work.

To accomplish this goal of assertiveness, especially in transitions, Rhonda needs to broaden her experience by drawing input (expanding Openness to Experience) from respected others about what specific approaches might be an effective balance between expectations of herself and others (modulating Agreeableness). For her, this type of issue can become an aspect of her style that she can master well (with her substantial Conscientiousness), or if not dealt with, this could become a step in the direction of eschewing all leadership opportunities. That type of foreclosure or at least moratorium would be unfortunate. The 3rd Language situation reoccurrence is usually avoidable.

Scenario 2

Scenario 2 involves Bart, a 40-year-old bank executive who has successfully transitioned from a branch manager to the director of the company's investment services division. Job-related stress, although substantial simply in terms of the amount and diversity of work, is not new to Bart nor is it in itself distressing. In fact, over time the obvious presence of high Conscientiousness and high Openness has been very instrumental in making Bart a good candidate for both advancement and increased specialization beyond the general banking skill set.

The interference for Bart is more internal and constitutional in the form of a susceptibility for depression. This is apparent in the high standards he sets for himself that would be difficult for most people to achieve regularly. Although that aspect of his personality contributes to difficulty in celebrating his work success, he comes from a family that is vulnerable for major depression. Bart had not experienced depression to any substantial degree since his senior year in college. At that time he was having difficulty resolving matters of uncertainty following graduation about what to do after the structural support of college was gone. Now at age 40, major depression had returned.

It is difficult to know exactly what causes major depression in any given situation. With Bart, the *stress diathesis model* probably applies as well as anything else. The diathesis concept is that Bart is predisposed by a genetically organized cluster of personality and biochemical characteristics to experience literally disabling levels of depressive discomfort. Both his parents had died in the last 18 months and he was struggling with middle-age adjustments. Both of these issues were factors in his depression. However, there was probably an element of the condition that was more purely biological in nature.

The disabling aspects of major depression are made known by a numbing lack of vitality, the presence of hopeless thoughts, a desire to shuns others' company, clouded concentration, and, in general, a desire to retreat from life. The sum of these elements form a significant road block to continuing normal life. In consultation with his family doctor and her social worker assistant, Bart agreed to begin a trial of antidepressants to regain his energy. He also committed to use the constructive thinking and behavioral activation strategies that the social worker gave him to get out of the negative, withdrawing hole of depression. The success rate with people who have Bart's profile history is quite high. For purposes of illustration, we can say he was pretty much back to his normal self within 90 days.

The 2nd Language strategy as applied to Bart is to applaud his having figured out by age 40 how to build on his Conscientiousness to establish mastery of his work life. He did this by keeping his options with other bank-related work opportunities, selecting those with greatest compatibility to himself, and successfully incorporating them in his professional skill set. For example, as a technical leader, he has been successful in developing structured training protocols for his subordinates that have aided them in accelerating through and mastering the basics of investment banking. Bart has essentially given his employees an opportunity to become competent, and the rewards for his diligence have been their great loyalty to him. What he has done is to import the problem-solving style that has kept him so functional as a professional into the skill-based training part of his job as supervisor of others. This application of his personality style has kept him reasonably satisfied with his progress over time, and has resulted in his being admired by others as a technical leader and good teacher of subordinates.

To be successful at work, Bart needs to be on top of his biological vulnerabilities as well as emerging trends in investment banking. If Bart had diabetes, he would need to manage his insulin or he would not be able to function. Similarly, within the overlapping Venn diagrams of a person, both in the world of work and in the world of health, Bart needs to use his Conscientiousness of follow through and his "heads-up" strengths with Openness to track when he is vulnerable to reoccurring depressive episodes. The conscientious attentiveness takes the form of seeing on your psychological radar screen events taking form in your life that will stimulate depressive experience or it may simply mean being vigilant to early signs of depression so that preventive strategies can be employed quickly.

Comment on Scenarios

From a developmental perspective, you can see that 2nd Language learning with Rhonda is directed toward using the discomfort of her work adjustment to refine her use of diligence as part of her Conscientiousness strength, augmented in the future with assertiveness as a key element in her Extraversion style. For Rhonda, the 3rd Language crisis became a 2nd Language learning opportunity. With Bart, who is much farther along the developmental path, the major depression event becomes a wake-up call to apply what has worked in his leadership style to his vulnerability for disabling affective disorders. In Scenario 1, the psychiatric condition gives way to 2nd Language learning. In Scenario 2, the 2nd Language strategy is employed to mitigate against relapsing into a psychiatric disorder.

Note on Personality Disorders

As you have read, we have presented a fairly optimistic view of 3rd Language scenarios and leadership development. This is despite the fact that the first author has been a professional psychologist and manager for 25 years. The rebuttal to this representation is that he has not adequately articulated the so-called "dark side of charisma" or taken into consideration the interference of personality disorders. It would be naive to say that there is no room for that type of discussion. However, it is open for discussion how often we view a pattern of behavior as a personality disorder as opposed to considering it the overemployment of what otherwise would be strengths if the circumstances were not so extreme.

The leader with high emotional stability, but rigidity in openness to new ideas about work patterns is not necessarily an obsessive personality, but rather a person who has enjoyed emotional health by being selective about which leadership responsibility he will adopt. The leader who is aggressive and bottom-line oriented may be considered by some to be a sociopath, yet, while needing to increase his concern for the welfare of individuals, he may actually being moving the business through a much-needed and difficult transition that will ultimately contribute to the security and common good of the whole workforce. It is important to keep in mind that personality disorders are defined by a rigid, continuous overemployment of a narrow set of problem-solving strategies that do not correlate well *both* in general functioning and with a specific problem situation.

With the target audience for this book—people predominantly in their 20s and 30s who are early or midterm in finding their way as leaders—we would err on the side of being overly optimistic that the rigid behavior they use and the distress they experience is more situational and symptomatic than reflective of a pervasive personality disorder.

What we would not want to miss and what may be missed, is the opportunity to offer the 2nd Language learning option to people who could continue in some aspect of leadership and make a contribution. Many of the people who are alleged failures as leaders are our failures, in not being able to see the broader opportunity to assist development within a leadership learning curve that we call learning the 2nd Language.

Please keep in mind that some leaders are malicious, beyond help and hope, and because of their deeply narcissistic, paranoid, and otherwise uncooperative and nonresponsive orientation, should not be leaders. You do not want to work for or with them, nor do any of us. People in positions of authority should not select them. However, that topic is one for another book, for someone else to write.

Individuation and Differentiation of the Three Languages

If we were to use a little poetic license to differentiate and connect the individuality of the three languages, we would call on the metaphors of weather and the daily inquiry from your loved one. In the weather frame, and with recognition that the authors are from the Seattle/Tacoma, Washington, area, the 1st Language is the bright, sunny day of untested, but situationally spectacular leadership success; the 2nd Language is an overcast day with sun breaks. The latter is the characteristic, more than acceptable Northwest experience complete with the daily challenges and incremental small victories (most of them only obvious to you, which is fine; count them up) of leadership. The 3rd Language is the dark night of snow and wind storms where the power is out indefinitely, with the despairing, painful realism of how inclement it can become when you foolishly put yourself in the zone of leadership. The meta-message to hold onto is that, like the weather, expect and learn to accept the full range of forecasts and climatic experience over the course of time while you are the leader.

As for the second metaphor, "How did today go?", if an individual is on the untested side of leadership, having mostly experienced 1st Language outcomes, a 2nd Language day was *not* a "good day." However, if he or she has been acclimated by a lot of 2nd Language learning and has recently endured a stormy, out-of-power experience with a 3rd Language event, then we would interpret a 2nd Language day as a triumph of being "back on my feet." The constant here is that your life is made up of ongoing days of leadership and the universal hope that we all evaluate our experience. Whereas through 2nd Language practice you can increase the dominance of 2nd Language competence, on the periphery of the bell-shaped curve of experience, you will intermittently encounter the intoxication of the 1st Language victory and the pain of the 3rd Language stumble.

A visual representation of the three languages of leadership can be found in Table 9.1. Included in the table is an identification of what it is (structure), what it does (function), and how to use it to your advantage (development implications).

TABLE 9.1
Overview of Leadership Experience, Structure, and Function

Leadership Experience	Structure	Function	Development Implication
1st Language	Personality strength	Superb when circumstances call for only or mostly your strength	Know when to draw from the strength; know when it will be insuffcient
2nd Language	Cogent use of personal strengths and weaknesses	Reliable, hardy strategy that will see you through a range of leadership situations	Use 2nd Language strategies by leveraging weakness(es) with strength(s); partner with others who complement you; choose not to pursue leadership opportunity if not compatible
3rd Language	Situational/pervasive dominance of personality weaknesses	Complex of personality and psychiatric problems present that cause moratorium or decline in leadership effectiveness	Acute side: reduce stress with professional assistance; maintenance side: emply 2nd Language approach as a strengthening and relapse prevention strategy

CLOSING COMMENTS

This chapter has been a bit divergent from the 2nd Language concept that is the predominant focus of the book. However, it is our intent to begin to connect the dots between 2nd Language thinking to the other obvious relationships. Accordingly, in this chapter we went beyond the usefulness of working with your personality strengths and weaknesses to build leadership effectiveness competence. We went on to discuss how to think about and deal with the related issue of psychiatric disturbance when you are a leader. We refer to dysfunctional behavior of leaders as the 3rd Language. Although far from a definitive statement about the issue, limiting the discussion as we did to the prevalence of these disorders, the vulnerabilities to them that we experience as leaders, and what can be done by way of professional help and 2nd Language strategies, we have at least opened up the topic.

Likewise, in the final chapter, we summarize the book's perspective on the question of how to go about receiving direct and practical 2nd Language training. The chapter provides ideas about what might be useful to you, based on the workshops concerning the 2nd Language of Leadership. We think you want a professional experience that is tailored to your questions. That type of very practical experience is not pushing somebody's pet theory on leadership. Instead, it involves your substantial participation, being completely confidential and for your use only.

Where We've Been and Where We're Going

Synopsis

This final chapter is a summary that takes you from our opening concern with the failure rate of leaders to the introduction of behavior change principles and personality data as an optional way to think about increasing leadership effectiveness. Employment of that option has included addressing and answering a series of questions. For example, how does personality in general, and the Big 5 in particular, help bridge the gap between a set of desired behaviors in understanding what it means to be an effective leader? Within the Big 5 framework, how can you leverage strengths to improve leadership using a strategy called the 2nd Language of Leadership? What are the tools available to augment the 2nd Language strategy? What can you do about leadership failures, especially when they include psychiatric problems?

In the aggregate, the 2nd Language approach, when it is tailored to you as an individual, can provide an opportunity for leaders to identify and develop effective behaviors. By way of the next steps, the features of a 2nd Language consultation product and how it can be accessed are described.

THE POPCORN CHRONICLES: AN ANALYSIS OF A CASE STUDY

As we reviewed the leaders' efforts in The Popcorn Chronicles case study to make the necessary organizational transitions, it became clear that a set of behavior patterns exists that increases the likelihood of success. Yet, given that these behaviors are based in our personalities, these strengths are unevenly distributed within and across people. Among the leadership strengths we all wish to have or at least to acquire, we drew five from the case study.

Effective leaders are great communicators. They are able to express themselves positively, listen intently as they translate information into action that activates people, and sort out what established information is useful and what new information must be added. As much as is reasonable, effective leaders value and incorporate the personal needs of the employees, as well as organizational goals; experience leadership challenges with minimal stress and highly adaptive behavior; and follow through with leadership responsibilities employing whatever personal and/or external resources that are necessary to accomplish the goals.

All these points offer guidance to any one of us who desires to increase our leadership effectiveness. However, they are not systematically organized, nor do they broadly characterize leadership and its relative importance in the world of work. To that end, leadership is defined as the process of making sense of situations and motivating people to accomplish goals consistent with whatever understandings you developed.

The work climate literature reveals that how well or poorly a leader lives that job description with one's team members will determine, more than any other variable, how satisfied workers are with their employment experience. Those of us in leadership roles are too often not considered to be functioning competently by our supervisees. And yes most, if not all of us, have felt less than competent at times, given the dynamic and ever-adjusting nature of the leadership role. However, the most relevant question here is what do leaders do that is recognized as desirable leadership?

FILLING IN THE GAPS OF EFFECTIVE LEADERSHIP: THE BIG 5

As workers across various industries describe effective leaders, a large number of behaviors are identified. These behaviors, framed as adjectives, converge with a personality theory that has come to be known as the Big 5 or the Five Factor approach (we will continue to use the name Big 5 as the encompassing title). The theory is conceptually compatible with both the experts' findings and my definition of leadership. The five factors are *Openness to Experience, Extraversion, Agreeableness, Adaptiveness* and *Conscientiousness*.

Bringing together the factors, the leadership definition, and the experts, we find that:

1. *Openness* is the process of evaluating current and past experience to make sense of a leadership situation.
2. *Extraversion* is the active well-roundedness of going to the world with your sense-making understandings, with the objective of activating others' interest in and engagement of this work.
3. *Agreeableness* is the registering of the other persons' motivational priorities, where you maximize efforts to link work objectives with personal objectives.
4. *Adaptiveness* is the perceptual ability to register leadership challenges with the least stress valence possible, so that you both experience for yourself and model to others that the work is doable and enabling.
5. *Conscientiousness* is the following through drawing from yours and others' diligence and commitment to do what it takes to get the job done.

Given that there is a conceptual advantage to being able to synthesize this information, related questions arise, such as why do so many leaders fail? Does the nature of personality aid or disadvantage us from increasing leadership effectiveness? What is the Big 5's history and which is the best personality test?

If you consider leadership effectiveness to be a set of behaviors that flow from our personalities, there are many leadership failures because we invariably come to the leadership role unprepared, without general coaching or education. Too often it is a coping exercise versus a mastery experience, with little recognition of our distortions of events and people, and where there is virtually no training that is individualized and focused on self-efficacy.

Whether information about desired leadership behavior may or may not be relevant depends on whether our personalities are malleable as opposed to fixed. The hard data shows that, at the trait level, our personality structures are crystallized by age 30. However, personality at the level of behaviors we choose and the life we lead are malleable within the trait structure. This means that there is room for maneuvering in desired directions without implying that one can or that it is desirable to modify personality significantly.

The Big 5 history flows from the work of a handful of contemporary psychologists who have been able to extract from our English language five domains of adjectives with similar meanings. More so than any other personality theory, the five domains accurately and consistently describe and predict people's behavior. Of the available Big 5 personality tests, the NEO–PI is the strongest. An abbreviated Big 5 measure called the Mini-Markers is available for your use in the Appendix.

INCREASING LEADERSHIP EFFECTIVENESS: CONNECTING THE BIG 5 AND THE 2ND LANGUAGE STRATEGY

The high ground of thinking about leadership effectiveness as basically equaling behaviors that flow out of personality (in this case, conceptualized as the Big 5) allows you to see the lay of the land of leadership in ways that were not so clear before. What you see are three levels of leadership. The first level is that of a perfect match between strength and situation. Whereas the feeling you get from this experience is very good, such alignment is not typical. What is more representative is working from a position of imperfect match between personal strength and situational leadership demand. Notice that there is quite a range in how well to poorly leaders work with this. Third, there is the level of leadership dysfunction, where the leader is failing in noteworthy ways in the endeavor of "making sense and motivating others." Often, this third level includes a psychiatric disorder.

We call these levels the three Languages of Leadership. The terminology of "language" is used both because the construct we use to describe leadership behavior is language, and because, of the three levels, the most important by far is the second one. Specifically, the 2nd Language of Leadership conveys figuratively and literally our key communication, that leadership is an acquired competency, not a natural one. No one is a 1st Language leadership star all the time, because no one has a perfect personality that always correlates with every leadership challenge.

By way of reinforcing the point, most of us in leadership were not selected or drawn to this "being in charge" assignment because we had a sense of the good fit between who we are as a person and the role. More often, the call to leadership came from some combination of senior leaders who were impressed with our potential, colleagues who believed that we had the ability to represent core work related values, and/or our technical skills and expertise were remarkable enough that the quasi-logical assumption was made that we would be a good leader, too.

None of these paths assures a successful passage to leadership. In fact, the strength of each of these beginnings, combined with the absence of truly understanding the larger job, can be and has been a formula for a bad outcome. Again the question surfaces, how can leadership failure be circumvented? Based on observations of 2nd Language performance, what strategies might be useful?

2nd Language Strategies

Today, the issue is often not so much whether there is enough information, but more often how to get it and how can we accept it. This is especially true with the 2nd Language of Leadership. To assist with the accessibility and acceptability of the Language of Leadership information, we review 2nd Language strategies that include enabling philosophies, effectiveness interventions, and the conceptual schema. Finally, we conclude with what we know about why and how people make behavioral changes.

A fundamental premise of the 2nd Language strategy is to know who you are, be able to accept that information, and work with it. What augments that outcome is the circumstance where leaders are respectfully appreciative of their personality strength and of the values that come alive when they lead a particular enterprise. For example, an individual can view one or more of her Big 5 domains as strong in the leadership equation, registering the powerful contribution she can make with being Open, Conscientious, well adjusted, and so on. Under those circumstances, it is much more likely that she can accept and work with the underpowered and interfering aspects of her style. Furthermore, if the work itself, whether it is the content, the customers, or the colleagues, carries great value and meaning to her, this can assist in coming to grips with her struggle as a leader. Such enabling philosophies make it possible to be sufficiently self-aware and confident enough to employ a 2nd Language intervention.

The effectiveness interventions are deceptively simple. The first option is to leverage strengths to improve or mitigate against the interference or weakness. For example, an individual might say, I will be conscientious [C] to be as interpersonally present [E], clear [O], emotionally comfortable [Adj], and straightforward [Agr] as is reasonable for me. Alternately, the intervention may include complementing this effort by partnering with those who balance these strengths and limitations. The third intervention is to be wise enough in an informed and sound way to choose not to lead in situations where the match between the leader and the requirements is not likely to work effectively.

To go full circle from the perspective of the enabling philosophies to implementing the interventions, a schema, implicitly or explicitly, needs to be followed. The steps in the schema are understanding the leadership situation, being clear about your personality, and recognizing how your personality predisposes a predictable range of behavior. In the case of leadership behavior, matching your reading of the situation and your personality and then employing the enabling philosophies and intervention tools that make up the 2nd Language strategy is the avenue to follow.

Our awareness of what is known about why people change and how they change makes this way of thinking about leadership effectiveness improvement an endeavor of optimism and hope. We know people change when they experience a sense of necessity, express a positive expectation that desired change can occur, and develop a tolerance that it is worthwhile to endure the relative discomforts of moving from the familiarity of the present to the greater effectiveness, yet unfamiliarity, of the future. A wealth of scientific study shows that behavior change happens best when it is focused and guided by a helpful, knowledgeable other.

The adult-education model clarifies that most of us participate in training like the 2nd Language strategy because we want to get answers to questions that are very practical matters for us. Given how people change, for an equal number of us, what we want is either information to hold for further consideration or action plans to put to immediate use. Goal setting is one form of action plan that is concrete and structured.

The 2nd Language strategy of increasing leadership effectiveness is a process of organizing and optimizing information and circumstances to accelerate learning that would occur for most leaders anyway, yet in a slower, more gradual way—provided they could survive the trial-and-error experience. The intent here is to assist you to anticipate as you enter the vestibule of leadership what you might expect and therefore anticipate around the corner in the way of challenges, based on your personality style. Without this assistance, the concern is that many will also become so discouraged, demoralized, and, yes, depressed that they will establish a moratorium on further leadership development or will leave the field of leadership together.

3rd Language of Leadership Failure

A secondary and much attenuated purpose of this book is to relate that although all of us have our 2nd Leadership challenges, many of us will experience the pain and discomfort of leadership failure. Often an aspect of that failure may be symptoms of a minor or major psychiatric disorder. We know that especially for leaders who are in the early to midcareer stage of their work lives, adjustments can be significantly challenging. The last 15 years of epidemiologic data have illuminated what has long been true, but not known. Depression and anxiety disorders are the common colds of life experience. These conditions are highly prevalent and can be quite distressing and disabling. Given the demands of being a leader, it is a safe bet that many leaders will experience work-related psychiatric disorders.

For those whose early or midterm forays into leadership yields psychiatric pain because of the mismatch between situational requirements and personality-based leadership skills, this is a singularly important leadership opportunity to learn 2nd Language adjustment. First, avail yourself of psychiatric assistance as necessary to control your pain so that you are not so distracted or derailed that learning becomes unnecessarily difficult. For those of you who have acquired substantial 2nd Language strengths, yet have become burdened with a major psychiatric disorder, in addition to receiving acute medical assistance, consider the use of 2nd Language strategies applied to your general life adjustment to assist in maintenance of well-being and prevention of a relapse.

CLOSING COMMENTS

Now that you have covered the terrain of first steps needed to get to the next steps, we want to pause to tell you of our deep appreciation that you have considered this 2nd Language perspective. Your interest is very gratifying.

The connection between the first steps and next steps is that although we do not know what you know about your personality and leadership effectiveness, we do know that the best we can do with a book is to introduce an idea. Most what has been offered is a broad brush conceptualizing of the 2nd Language idea. The next steps address how to move you, when you choose, to a knowledge of more specific personal information and potential action directions.

Because both of us speak from experience due our professional training and careers, we know that what works best with people learning new behavior is to make sure that all the ingredients of the following behavior change recipe are present. It is important, first and foremost, to get a sample of your behavior. The 2nd Language Questionnaire and the NEO–PI are examples. It is valuable to know what implicit or explicit theories of leadership you espouse. We have offered a very broad one with the sense-making/people-motivating notion. Whatever changes you make, you will want to work within or from your own personal theory. Finally, because you are a leader, engaged in influencing the order of events around you, you will want to be actively involved and preferably direct any leadership improvement initiative.

What follows is a description of the generic features of offering you a 2nd Language consultation. It can be offered as stand-alone one-to-one feedback to you drawing from the NEO–PI and the 2nd Language Questionnaire, or it may be part of a workshop for a group that would also include the separate one-to-one consultation.

PRODUCT FEATURES

The 2nd Language product is easy to access, convenient to your schedule, reliably and professionally produced packages of assessment and training services. It is designed to increase your leadership effectiveness at work in ways that make sense to you.

What the 2nd Language Product Is

- An action-oriented, skill-based training program for highly motivated people with potential for increasing their leadership effectiveness.
- Adult-education-oriented with emphasis on participants determining what it is about their personality they would like to understand better as a means to increase their leadership effectiveness.
- Focused on accelerating normal development of leadership effectiveness skills.
- Geared for entry and midterm leaders.

- Offered by professionals knowledgeable in applied psychology and business.
- Empirically based in its assessment and training components.
- Directed toward mastery, building on your skills and values, and completely confidential.

What the 2nd Language Product Is Not

- A clinical or in any way a health-care-oriented activity.
- A career or vocational service.
- A pedagogical process where an instructor decides what is to be taught and how it is to be learned.
- A coping skill or stress-management program.
- A motivational program.
- Based on a particular school of thought about leadership effectiveness.
- A team-building or organizational-development service, although these may be by-products.
- Owned by or accessible to anyone but you.

Appendix

2ND LANGUAGE OF LEADERSHIP QUESTIONNAIRE

1. Describe your current leadership position. What it is? How many people do you supervise? How long you have been in the role? What are the duties?
2. Please give an example from your own personal experience of successful use of self in a leadership role. I am specifically asking you to give an example where you needed to make sense of a situation and then work with your team to get a job done.
3. Provide a brief description of a leadership situation that significantly challenged you in your use of self, and where you felt you could and would like to improve your performance.
4. How long of a history do you have of functioning in formal (title and responsibility as the boss) and/or informal (i.e., as in opinion leader, not in charge but the person people look up to) leadership roles? Please give examples and identify how satisfied you have been with your performance.
5. Concerning leadership roles, please respond to whether you see yourself:
   - trying it out as a new experience,
   - deepening or fine-tuning your skills in an established area or possibly a new endeavor, or
   - finding the work frustrating, but willing to try it a bit longer?
6. Describe your circumstances so you will have confidence that I understand your situation.
7. What goals are important to you in your role as a leader? How do you see both your personal strengths and your vulnerabilities impacting your accomplishing these goals?
8. Beyond what you have read here, or have become aware of in any other way, what are your expectations of this consultation?

Signature _____ Date _____

APPENDIX 115

40-ITEM MINI-MARKER INSTRUMENT

How Accurately Can You Describe Yourself?

Use the list of common human traits shown to describe yourself as accurately as possible. Think about how you see yourself generally or typically at the present time, not as you wish to be in the future. Describe yourself as compared with other persons you know of the same sex and roughly your same age.

Before each trait, write a number indicating how accurately that trait describes you, using the following rating scale.

	Inaccurate						Accurate		
	Extremely	Very	Moderately	Slightly	Uncertain	Slightly	Moderately	Very	Extremely
	1	2	3	4	5	6	7	8	9

	Column 1	Column 2	Column 3	Column 4
Row 1	____Talkative	____Extraverted	____Bold	____Energetic
Row 2	____Cold	____Rude	____Unsympathetic	____Harsh
Row 3	____Efficient	____Practical	____Systematic	____Organized
Row 4	____Moody	____Temperamental	____Jealous	____Fretful
Row 5	____Complex	____Creative	____Philosophical	____Imaginative
Row 6	____Withdrawn	____Shy	____Bashful	____Quiet
Row 7	____Kind	____Sympathetic	____Warm	____Cooperative
Row 8	____Sloppy	____Inefficient	____Careless	____Disorganized
Row 9	____Envious	____Touchy	____Unenvious	____Relaxed
Row 10	____Deep	____Intellectual	____Uncreative	____Unintellectual

Scoring

Step 1: Add the numbers of the four columns across each row you selected and place the totals in the blanks below. Note specific instructions for adding numbers from Rows 9 and 10.

Row 1 ____
Row 2 ____
Row 3 ____
Row 4 ____
Row 5 ____

Row 6 ____
Row 7 ____
Row 8 ____
Row 9 (Columns 1 & 2 ____) (Columns 3 & 4 ____)
Row 10 (Columns 1 & 2 ____) (Columns 3 & 4 ____)

Step 2: Proceed with the following calculations to derive the five factors.

Factor I   Row 1 ____ – Row 6 ____ = ____ + 40 = ____ ÷ 8 = ____
Factor II   Row 7 ____ – Row 2 ____ = ____ + 40 = ____ ÷ 8 = ____
Factor III Row 3 ____ – Row 8 ____ = ____ + 40 = ____ ÷ 8 = ____
Factor IV Columns 3 & 4 Row 9 ___ – Row 4 ___ = ___ – Columns 1 & 2 Row 9 ___ + 60 – ___ ÷ 8 = ___
Factor V   Columns 1 & 2 Row 10 ___ + Row 5 ___ = ___ – Columns 3 & 4 Row 10 ___ + 20 – ___ ÷ 8 ___

Step 3: Labeling the factors.

Factor I is Extraversion
Factor II is Agreeableness
Factor III is Conscientiousness
Factor IV is Emotional Stability (aka Neuroticism)
Factor V is Intellect/Imagination (aka Openness to Experience)

Step 4: Interpreting your scores with community norms.

The scores from the five factors can now be compared to those from the community sample summarized in Table A.1, which are 1993 norms that were derived from a sample of 1,125 community residents of Eugene–Springfield, Oregon. Keep in mind that the Mini-Marker instrument is a very broad representation of personality; being "average" means literally that you are in general like most people concerning one of the five major traits. Conversely, if your score varies by one or more standard deviations from the average, you are respectively very low, low, high or very high in strength relative to the trait. The scores for each factor are the average of the responses on a scale from 1 to 9.

MINI-MARKER SCORING EXAMPLE

The following explanation walks you through a Mini-Marker scoring from start to finish so you will have a reference for your own scoring. Our sample individual has the following scores:

Factor I—Extraversion

Row 1: Talkative 5, Extraverted 6, Bold 7, Energetic 8 = Sum of 26
Row 6: Withdrawn 2, Shy 2, Bashful 4, Quiet 5 = Sum of 13
Calculated that is: (26 – 13) = 13 + 40 = 53 ÷ 8 = 6.6

By consulting Table A.2, the 6.6 score reflects that in general this person is not high, but is nonetheless above average in Extraversion. You see some indication, however, that this person sees himself as more energetic

APPENDIX

TABLE A.1
Community Sample of Scores

Factors	Very Low	Low	Average	High	Very High
I. Extraversion	3.08	4.39	5.70	7.01	8.32
II. Agreeableness	5.60	6.46	7.32	8.18	9.04
III. Conscientiousness	4.50	5.62	6.74	7.86	8.98
IV. Emotional Stability	3.43	4.61	5.79	6.97	8.15
V. Intellect/Imagination	4.37	5.46	6.55	7.64	8.73

Note. These norms apply to the 9-point rating scale used in self ratings. The respective standard deviations were Factor I: (1.31), Factor II: (0.86), Factor III: (1.12), Factor IV: (1.18), Factor V: (1.09).

The designation of Average means that out of a theoretical 100 people, most people would score about average and 50% would be above and below this number. Low means that this is the value which falls one standard deviation below the average, and that roughly 84% of the population scores higher; Very Low, two standard deviations below the average, 98% of the population scores higher. From the opposite direction, High is one standard deviation above the average meaning that only 14% of the population would have a higher score; Very High means two standard deviations above average, only 2% score higher.

Most people are average in their endorsements of how much a factor is representative of them. As one moves out from Average to Low or High, relatively fewer people show this range or endorsement. Very Low and Very High are even less common. Appreciation is extended to Gerard Saucier (1994) for making this information available.

than social. This type of differentiation, based on a numerical score, is not possible in a precise way with the Mini-Markers.

Factor II—Agreeableness

> Row 7: Kind 7, Sympathetic 7, Warm 6, Cooperative 6 = Sum of 26
> Row 2: Cold 2, Rude 2, Unsympathetic 2, Harsh 2 = Sum of 8
> Calculated that is: $(26 - 8) = 18 + 40 = 58 \div 8 = 7.25$

Again referring to Table A.1, 7.25 is slightly below average. Yet this is so close to 7.32, the sample average, that it is accurate to say that this person evaluates himself about average on the Agreeableness trait. The rankings of the adjectives suggest that the individual is a caring person although not demonstrative.

Factor III—Conscientiousness

> Row 3: Efficient 8, Practical 7, Systematic 7, Organized 8 = Sum of 30
> Row 8: Sloppy 2, Inefficient 2, Careless 2, Disorganized 2 = Sum of 8
> Calculated that is: $(30 - 8) = 22 + 40 = 62 \div 8 = 7.75$

With Factor III, we observe rankings that uniformly indicate that the Conscientiousness characteristic is very representative across the board. The positive set of the first four adjectives received very accurate self-ratings, whereas the adjectives that are the opposite of Conscientiousness have received very inaccurate self-ratings. It is intuitively and quantitatively right to conclude that this person perceives himself as strong and high in Conscientiousness.

Factor IV—Emotional Stability

> Row 9—Columns 3 & 4: Relaxed 3, Unenvious 7 = Sum of 10
> Row 4: Moody 3, Temperamental 2, Jealous 3, Fretful 4 = Sum of 12
> Row 9—Columns 1 & 2: Envious 2, Touchy 3 = Sum of 5
> Calculated that is: $(10 - 12 - 5) = -7 + 60 = 53 \div 8 = 6.6$

Notice that six of the eight adjectives refer to a lack of Emotional Stability. This is in contrast to the previous three factors where the breakdown between those adjectives that do and do not track with the trait are evenly matched. From a descriptive point of view, this person is above average in emotional stability, meaning the individual is even-tempered and not prone toward being threatened by or envious of others. On the other hand, rankings on specific adjectives like Relaxed and Fretful raise questions about response style related to experience of anxiety and frustration tolerance.

Factor V—Intellect/Imagination

> Row 10—Columns 1 & 2: Deep 7, Intellectual 7 = Sum of 14
> Row 5: Complex 8, Creative 6, Philosophical 8, Imaginative 5 = Sum of 27
> Row 10—Columns 3 & 4: Uncreative 3, Unintellectual 2 = Sum of 5
> Calculated that is: $(14 + 27 - 5) = 36 + 20 = 56 \div 8 = 7$

This factor has been structured in direct contrast to the previous one. The rankings are in the direction of strength as you will notice with the first six adjectives, plus they are all added together (as opposed to subtracted with Factor 4). Accordingly, the sum of the rankings for the first six adjectives subtracted from the last two is added to 20 (vs. 40 or 60), in order to maintain a relative value with the computations on the other factors. As you will notice using Table A.1 as a guide, this person is about mid-point between average and high on Intellect. You could surmise that the person experiences him or herself as a thinker who can see the world in its complexity, yet does not see himself as principally an innovator. In other words, the individual understands the world in depth, but doesn't typically create new things.

SUMMARY

The person's overall profile indicates Extraversion; Agreeableness, and Emotional Stability are average, and Conscientiousness and Intellect/Imagination are high. This person's uniform greatest strength is Conscientious follow-through. Although also emotionally hardy and resilient, he may experience challenges in managing restlessness, anxiety, and frustrating circumstances. This is probably mitigated by his active, energetic style, which we can infer because his first factor is more achievement-oriented in motivation than principally organized around being socially outgoing. He cares about people, but is far from showy in his affections. Understanding complexity seems to come naturally, although he doesn't consider himself to be especially creative.

From a leadership perspective, the key issues to be aware of are that this is a person who follows through in an active, thoughtful, and typically emotionally steady way. A study of individual items could raise questions about very specific areas of possible interference to the leadership work of making sense of situations and motivating others. The questions would be addressed to issues of social introversion, anxiety threshold, and ability to express credible concern for others.

With the Mini-Markers, it is important to emphasize that it is not possible to confirm with this little information whether these questions are indeed issues, or, if they are, whether they are matters that can be successfully managed. A more complete picture of the individual is not possible without a more detailed measure like the NEO–PI and more personal and contextual information.

References

Agency for Health Care Policy and Research: Depression in primary care: Detention, diagnosis, and treatment. (1993). *U.S. Department of Health and Human Services, 5*, 1–21.

Ankuta, G., & Abeles, N. (1993). Client satisfaction, clinical significance, and meaningful change in psychotherapy. *Professional Psychology: Research and Practice, 24*(1), 70–74.

Ash, M. K. (1984). *Mary Kay on people management*. New York: Warner Books.

Baron, R. A., & Byrne, D. (1991). *Social psychology: Understanding human interactions* (6th ed., 571–573) Boston: Allyn and Bacon.

Barrick, M. R., & Mount, M. K. (1991). The big five personality dimensions and job performance: A meta-analysis. *Personnel Psychology, 44*, 1–26.

Bass, B. M. (1990). From transactional to transformational leadership: Learning to share the vision. *Organizational Dynamics, 18*, 19–31.

Bass, B. M. (1998). *Tranformational leadership*. Mahwah, NJ: Lawrence Erlbaum Associates.

Broadhead, W., Blazer, D., & George, L. (1992). Depression, disability days and days lost from work in a prospective epidemiologic survey. *Journal of the American Medical Association, 267*, 1478–1483.

Budman, S. H., & Armstrong, E. (1992, Fall). Training for managed care settings: How to make it happen. *Psychotherapy, 29*(3), 416–421.

Bunker, K. A., & Webb, A. D. (1992). *Learning how to learn from experience: Impact of stress and coping* (Center for Creative Leadership, Rep. Number 154).

Cloninger, C. R., Dragan, M. S., & Przybeck, T. R. (1993). A psychobiological model of temperment and character. *Archives of General Psychiatry, 50*(12), 975–990.

Cooley, J. C., & Impara, J. P. (Eds.). (1995). *12th mental measurements yearbook*. Lincoln, NE: Buros Institute and University of Nebraska Press.

Conner, D. R. (1992). *Managing at the speed of change*. New York: Random House.

REFERENCES

Costa, P. T., Jr., & McCrae, R. R. (1992). *Revised NEO personality inventory (NEO-PI-R) and NEO five-factor inventory (NEO-FFI) professional manual.* Odessa, FL: Psychological Assessment Resources.

Costa, P. T., Jr., & McCrae, R. R. (1994). *NEO PI-R: Bibliography for the revised NEO personality inventory and NEO five factor inventory.* Odessa, FL: Psychological Assessment Resources.

Costa, P. T., Jr., & McCrae, R. R. (1995). Domains and facets: Hierarchical personality assessment using the revised NEO personality inventory. *Journal of Personality Assessment, 64*(1), 21–50.

Costa, P. T., Jr., & McCrae, R. R. (1997). Stability and change in personality assessment: The revised NEO personality inventory in the year 2000. *Journal of Personality Assessment, 68*(1), 86–94.

Covey, S. (1989). *The 7 habits of highly effective people.* New York: Simon & Schuster.

Digman, J. M. (1990). Personality structure: The emergence of the five-factor model. In M. R. Rosenzweig & L. W. Porter (Eds.), *Annual review of psychology,* (Vol. 41, pp. 417–440). Palo Alto, CA: Annual Reviews.

Digman, J. M. (1996). The curious history of the five-factor model of personality. In J. S. Wiggins (Ed.), *The five-factor model of personality: Theoretical perspectives.* New York: Guilford.

Fielder, F. E. (1967). *A theory of leadership effectiveness.* New York: McGraw-Hill.

Fielder, F. E. (1992). Time-based measures of leadership experience and organizational performance: A review of research and preliminary model. *Leadership Quarterly, 3*(1), 5–23.

Goldberg, L. R. (1993). The structure of phenotypic personality traits. *American Psychologist, 48,* 26–34.

Goleman, D. (1995). *Emotional intelligence.* New York: Bantam.

Guest, C. (1999, June 11). Talk about a power perk: Mary Kay's pink Cadillac. *The Kansas City Business Journal, 17,* p. 15.

Hanna, F. J., & Ritchie, M. H. (1995). Seeking the active ingredients of psychotherapeutic change: Within and outside the context of therapy. *Professional Psychology: Research and Practice, 26*(2), 176–183.

Hogan, R., Curphy, G. J., & Hogan, J. (1994, June). What we know about leadership, effectiveness and personality. *American Psychologist, 49*(6), 493–504.

House, R. J., & Howell, J. M. (1992). Personality and charismatic leadership. *Leadership Quarterly, 3*(2), 81–108.

Howard, K. I., Kopta, S. M., Krause, M. S., & Orlinsky, D. E. (1986, February). The dose–effect relationship in psychotherapy. *American Psychologist, 41*(2), 159–164.

Hughes, R. L., Ginnett, R. C., & Curphy, G. J. (1996). *Leadership: Enhancing the lessons of experience.* Chicago: Irwin.

Johnson, J., Weissman, M., & Klerman, G. (1992). Service utilization and social morbidity associated with depressive symptoms in the community. *Journal of the American Medical Association, 267,* 1478–1483.

Katon, W., Von Korff, M., & Lin E. (1990). Distressed high utilizers of medical care: DSM-II diagnosis and treatment needs. *General Hospital Psychiatry, 2,* 355–362.

Kouzes, J. M., & Posner, B. Z. (1997). *The leadership challenge.* San Francisco: Jossey-Bass.

Levinson, D. J. (1986). A conception of adult development. *American Psychologist, 41*(1), 3–13.

Levinson, D. J., & Levinson, J. (1996). *The seasons of a woman's life*. New York: Knopf.
Levinson, D. J., Darrow, C. M., Klein, E. B., Levinson, M. H., & McKee. (1978). *The seasons of a man's life*. New York: Ballantine Books.
Lipsey, M. W., & Wilson, D. B. (1993). The efficacy of psychological, educational, and behavioral treatment: Confirmation from meta-analysis. *American Psychologist, 48*(12), 1181–1209.
Locke, E., & Latham, G. P. (1984). *Goal setting: A motivational technique that works!* Englewood Cliffs, NJ: Prentice Hall.
Locke, E., Shaw, K., Saari, L., & Latham, G. P. (1981). Goal setting and task performance 1969–1980. *Psychological Bulletin, 90*, 125–152.
Mabe, P. A., & West, S. G. (1992). Validity of self-evaluation of ability: A review and meta-analysis. *Journal of Applied Psychology, 67*, 280–296.
MacDonald, K. (1995). Evolution, the five-factor model, and levels of personality. *Journal of Personality, 63*, 3.
McAdams, D. P. (1994). Can personality change? Levels of stability and growth in personality across the life span. In T. F. Heatherton & J. L. Weinberger (Eds.), *Can personality change?* (pp. 299–314). Washington, DC: American Psychological Association.
McCrae, R. R., & Costa, P. T. (1990). *Personality in adulthood*. New York: Guilford.
McNeilly, C. L., & Howard, K. H. (1991). The effects of psychotherapy: A reevaluation based on dosage. *Psychotherapy Research, 1*(1), 74–78.
Millon, T. (1990). *Toward a new personology: An evolutionary model*. New York: Wiley.
Mintzberg, H. (1994, Fall). Rounding out the manager's job. *Sloan Management Review*, 11–26.
Murphy, E. C. (1996). *Leadership IQ*. New York: Wiley.
Piedmont, R. L. (1998). *The revised NEO personality inventory: Clinical and research applications*. New York: Plenum Press.
Platt, C. (1995, May). Beats skinning hogs. *Wired*, pp. 3, 161–215.
Prochaska, J. O., Norcross, J. C., & DiClemente, C. C. (1994). *Changing for good*. New York: William Morrow.
Prochaska, J. O., DiClemente, C. L., & Norcross, J. C. (1992). In search of how people change. Applications to addictive behaviors. *American Psychologist, 47*(9), 1102–1114.
Regier, D., Goldberg, D., & Taube, O. (1978). The defacto U.S. mental health services system: A public health perspective. *Archives of General Psychiatry, 38*, 685–693.
Roberson, L. (1990). Prediction of job satisfaction from characteristics of personal work goals. *Journal of Organizational Behavior, 11*, 29–41.
Rose, R. (1995). Genes and human behavior. *Annual Review of Psychology, 46*, 625–654.
Saucier, G. (1994). Mini-makers: A brief version of Goldberg's unipolar big-five markers. *Journal of Personality Assessment, 63*(3), 506–516.
Saucier, G., & Goldberg, L. R. (1996). The language of personality: Lexical perspectives of the five-factor model. In J. S. Wiggins (Ed.), *The five factor model of personality: Theoretical perspectives*. New York: Guilford.
Schlender, S. (1998, November 9). The three faces of Steve. *Fortune*, pp. 96–103.
Schultz, H., & Yang, D. J. (1997). *Pour your heart into it*. New York: Hyperion.

REFERENCES

Shapiro, S., Skinner, E., & Kramer, M. (1985). Measuring need for mental health services in a general population. *Medical Care, 23*, 1033–1043.

Simon, G., & Von Korff, M. (1995). Recognition, management and outcomes of depression in primary care. *Archives of Family Medicine, 4*, 99–105.

Smith, M. L., Glass, G. V., & Miller, T. I. (1980). *The benefits of psychotherapy*. Baltimore: Johns Hopkins University Press.

Stogdill, R. M. (1948). Personal factors associated with leadership: A survey of the literature. *Journal of Psychology, 25*, 35–71.

Stogdill, R. M. (1963). *Manual for the leader behavior description questionnaire form XII*. Columbus: Ohio State University, Bureau of Business Research.

Tziner, A., & Latham, G. P. (1989). The effects of appraisal instrument, feedback and goal-setting on worker satisfaction and commitment. *Journal of Organizational Behavior, 10*, 145–153.

Von Korff, M., & Simon, G. (1996, December). The prevalence and impact of psychological disorders in primary care: HMO research needed to improve care. *HMO Practice, 10*(4), 150–155.

Warshaw, M. (1997, March). Guts and glory. *Success*, pp. 28–33.

Wells, K., Steward, A., & Hays, R. (1988). The functioning and well-being of depressed patients. *Journal of the American Medical Association, 262*, 914–919.

Willis, G. (1994). *Certain trumpets: The call of leaders*. New York: Simon & Schuster.

Yukl, G. (1989). Managerial leadership: A review of theory and research. *Journal of Management, 15*(2), 251–289.

Yukl, G. (1998). *Leadership in organizations* (4th ed.). Upper Saddle River, NJ: Prentice Hall.

Yukl, G., & Van Fleet, D. D. (1996). Theory and research on leadership organizations. In M. D. Dunnette & L. M. Hough (Eds.), *Handbook of industrial & organizational psychology* (2nd ed., Vol. 3, pp. 147–198.). Palo Alto, CA: Consulting Psychology Press.

Index

1st Language of Leadership, xiii, 39, 40, 41, 47, 49, 50, 95
    Paradigm shift view, 41
    Power view, 41, 42–43
    Social view, 41, 43
    Transformational view, 41, 42
2nd Language of Leadership, ix, x, 37, 39, 40, 43, 44, 46, 47, 50, 51, 52, 54, 95, 102–106, 109
    high-achieving leader, 51, 53–55
    popular leader, 51, 55–56
    technical/expert leader, 51, 57–59
        product features, 112–113
        Questionnaire, xii, 112, 114
        schema, 61, 73, 110
3rd Language of Leadership, xiii, 39, 40, 47, 48, 49, 50, 95, 102–105, 111
    vulnerabilities of leaders, 97–105
Adult education, 81–82, 110
Apple Computer, 47, 48
Ash, Mary Kay, 41, 43
Barrick and Mount, 18
Bass, Bernard, xi
BENCHMARKS, 22
Big 5, 19, 31–37, 52, 107–108
    Adaptiveness, 18, 34, 107–108
    Agreeableness, 17, 32, 34, 107–108
    Conscientiousness, 18, 32, 34, 107–108
    Emotional stability, 36
    Extraversion, 17, 26, 32, 34, 107–108
    framework for, xiii
    history, 32, 108
    Neuroticism, 18, 32, 36
    Openness, 16, 32, 33, 34, 36, 107–108
    structure, xii
    theory of personality, ix, xi, 16
Bunker, 18
Bush, George, 52
Center for Creative Leadership, xi
Center for Health Studies, 97
Change, 78
    how people, 78 – 82
    personal characteristics, 78
Character, 20
Churchill, Winston, 72
Circumplex model, 68
Clinton, Bill, 52, 62, 64
Cloninger, 20
Costa and McCrae, 26, 28, 32, 34, 35
Counseling, 23, 75–77
Covey, Steven, 70
Defense mechanisms, 63
Digman, John, 32
Domains, 34

INDEX

Doonesbury, 52
Einstein, Albert, xi
Eisenhower, 72
Emotional intelligence, 20
Emergent leadership, 20
Empirical leadership, 20
Enabling philosophies, 61
Epidemiological Catchment Area study, 96
Facets, 34
Fiedler, 16
Five Factor Model, 19, 32, 107
Freud, 31, 76
Frustration–aggression hypothesis, 79
Gates, Bill, 41, 42
Goal Outcome Matrix (GOM), 84, 88–92
Goal Process Matrix (GPM), 84, 92–94
Goal setting, 85
   defined, 84
   purpose of, 85–86
   SMART, 86–88, 89
Goldberg and Digman, 34
Goldberg, Lew, 32, 35
Goleman, Daniel, 20
Graham, Martha, 41, 43
Hitler, Adolf, 47
Hobbes, Thomas, 79
Hogan, Robert, 14, 15
Howard, Ken, 77
Hypothetical construct, 20
Imagination, 37
Implicit leadership, 20
Intellect, 37
Intervention options, 67, 109
James, William, 79
Jobs, Steven, 47, 48, 49
JoHari Window, 23
Jones, Jim, 47
Jung, 31
Kennedy, John F., 71
King, Martin Luther, Jr., 41, 42
Leader–manager debate, 9
Leader
   expert, 57
   high-achieving, 55, 56, 69
   popular, 51, 55–56, 70
   unsuccessful, 21–24
Leadership, see also 1st, 2nd, 3rd
   behavioral aspects of, 9
   definition of, xii, 14–15, 107
   development strategies, 60
   conceptual schema, 60, 73–74
   effectiveness interventions, 60, 67–73
   enabling philosophies, 60–65
   dysfunctional, 96
   effectiveness and the Big 5, 16
   emergent, 20
   empirical, 20
   implicit, 20
   psychiatric conditions in, 96–97
Leadership effectiveness and the Big 5, 16
   Agreeableness, 17–18
   Conscientiousness, 18–19
   Extraversion, 17
   Neuroticism (Adaptiveness), 18
   Openness, 16–17
Leary, Timothy, 68
Levinson, Daniel, 27, 98
Levels of personality, 28–30
Lipsey and Wilson, 77
Managing at the Speed of Change, xi
McAdams, Dan, 26, 28, 29
Medical Outcome Studies, 96
Mental Measurement Year Book, 33
Mentoring, 63
Millon, Ted, 97
Mini-Markers, xi, xii, 33, 35, 36, 38, 74, 108, 115
Minnesota Multiphasic Personality Inventory, xi, 22, 31
PROFILOR, 22
Mintzberg, 17
Myers–Briggs, xi, 22
National Institute of Mental Health, 96
NEO-PI, xi, 26, 32, 33, 34, 35, 36, 37, 38, 44, 46, 52, 54, 74, 108
   critical review of, 33
   reliability, 33
   summary, 56, 58
   validity, 33
NeXt Corporation, 48
Nixon, Richard, 47, 49
Paradigm Shift View, 42
Persian Gulf war, 41
Personality,
   change, 25–29
   disorders, 102
   levels of, 28–30
Personality theories, 30
   classification of theories, 30
   Assessment, 30–31

Empirical, 30–31
School of thought, 30–31
Picasso, Pablo, 42
Pixar Animation Studios, 48
Popcorn Chronicles, 1, 9, 17, 18, 106–107
Powell, Colin, 72
Power view, 41–43
Psychological Assessment Resources, 34
Pygmalion, 78
Rand, 96
Reagan, Nancy, 71
Reagan, Ronald, 52
Roosevelt, Eleanor, 41, 71
Roosevelt, Franklin D., 71
Saucier, Gerard, 34–35, 36, 117
Schema, 61, 73, 110
Schultz, Howard, 41, 43
Schwarkopf, Norman, 41
Skinner, B.F., 31
SMART goals, 86
Smith and Glass, 76
Social View, 43
Stalin, Josef, 47
Starbucks, 43
Stogdill, 19
Stress diathesis model, 101
SYMLOG, 22
The Leadership Challenge, xi
The Limited, Inc., 42
Transactional leadership, xi
Transformational leadership, xi
Transformational View, 42
The Seasons of a Man's Life, 27, 98
The Seasons of a Woman's Life, 27, 98
Trudeau, Gary, 52
U.S. Post Office, 2
Waitt, Ted, 33
Wall Street Journal, 6
Watergate, 49
Wexner, Leslie, 41, 42
Wills, Gary, 71
Woody Allen, 8
YAVIS syndrome, 78